AFRICAN ART

AFRICAN ART
AN INTRODUCTION

FRANK WILLETT

Praeger Publishers
New York · Washington

BOOKS THAT MATTER

Published in the United States of America in 1971
by Praeger Publishers, Inc.
111 Fourth Avenue, New York, N.Y.10003

Library of Congress Catalog Card Number: 76–117394

Printed and bound in Great Britain

*For my very good friend William Fagg
who first taught me to deepen my enjoyment of
African art by increasing my understanding of it*

Contents

CHAPTER ONE
Introducing Africa   9

CHAPTER TWO
The Development of the Study of African Art   27

CHAPTER THREE
Towards a History of African Art   43

    Drawings and Paintings on Rock   43
    Ancient Sculpture   65
    European Sources of African Art History   80
    Egypt in Africa   109

CHAPTER FOUR
African Architecture   115

CHAPTER FIVE
Looking at African Sculpture   139

CHAPTER SIX
Understanding African Sculpture   161

CHAPTER SEVEN
African Art Today   239

Notes   267

Bibliography   275

Acknowledgments   281

Index   283

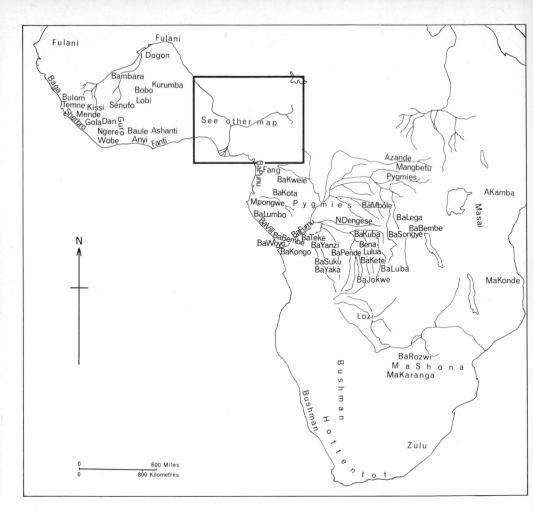

1A Peoples referred to in the text.

NOTE

Bantu names are used in English both with and without their prefix. In this book they are usually quoted with the prefix, and a capital letter is used to indicate the root, *e.g.* BaKwele. However in a few cases in which the root form only is in common use I have employed this form, *e.g.* Zulu rather than AmaZulu. The bibliography however quotes the form given by the individual author.

CHAPTER ONE

Introducing Africa

There already exists a considerable literature on African art, much of it more valuable for its illustrations than its text. The most significant studies are generally those of limited scope, dealing with the art of a single society or area. Books and articles of this kind do not usually have wide distribution, and the general reader sees only books (like this one!) which deal with the art of the whole continent. Most of these share the major characteristic of making general statements about Africa as if this vast and varied continent were a homogeneous

18 Peoples and places in and near Nigeria.

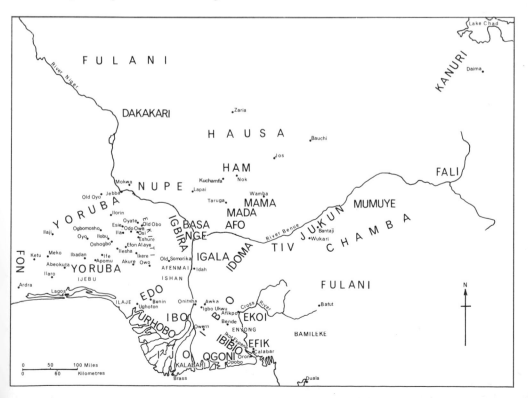

unit. Translated into statistical terms they have the effect of such assertions as that the average African family consists of one husband, one and a half wives and four and three-quarter children.[1] Many of the generalizations that have been made about African art, artists or societies do not have comparable danger-signals built into them, so it is advisable to view all such declarations with scepticism.

The mere size of the African continent indicates the dangers of generalization. Its area of twelve million square miles is more than three times that of the United States, including Alaska. The United States could be superimposed on the Sahara desert and not touch the coast of Africa at any point. Its population is about 240 millions, living mostly at densities below twenty-five to the square mile; it is only in part because such vast areas are so thinly populated that it has more distinct peoples and cultures than any other continent. Its coastal plains are relatively narrow so that although the great rivers are navigable for immense distances in the interior, they often plunge off the plateaux with cataracts and rapids (the Victoria Falls on the Zambesi are 343 feet high, twice as high as Niagara, and the flow of water over the Stanley Falls on the Congo is twice that of Niagara) and they end up in great deltas, rather than in navigable estuaries. Only the West Mediterranean coast affords good harbours. In consequence, direct external influences, apart from the Cretan ones in the late second millennium BC and those resulting from the Assyrian invasion of Egypt in 666 BC (the latter of which seems to have had very little cultural effect in any case) were for a long time limited to the coasts, though trade goods found their way inland. Penetration of foreigners into the interior came only after the Industrial Revolution, when Europe was seeking sources of raw materials and markets for the finished goods. Today, with all kinds of communication in operation, no part of Africa is entirely out of touch with the rest of the world, and the materialistic values of Western society, which are its easiest to export, are almost everywhere replacing the traditional spiritual ones. African societies are changing and so are their arts, which are reflecting increasingly, even though often unconsciously, the new values.

Some of the most persistent stereotyped misconceptions about Africa concern the physical environment. The entire continent is commonly visualized as covered with jungle (a word which is never used in an African context) or with desert. In fact, there is a gradation from one to the other. Desert is found, of course, in the Sahara, in the margin of the Horn (the easternmost point), and in the Kalahari to the south. Yet these are not areas of bare sand; nine-tenths of them are covered with scattered scrub vegetation. The tropical rain forest (known as 'jungle' in southern Asia and 'selvas' in South America) is quite limited in extent. It is found along the West African or Guinea Coast (with an important gap in Togo and Dahomey), Cameroun, Gabon, Congo-Brazzaville and the northern part of Congo-Kinshasa. There is a separate patch of forest on the east coast of Madagascar. On the east and south of the rain forest, which as its name implies is in the area of heaviest rainfall (more than sixty inches a year), we find the dry forest. The forest edges everywhere grade through a forest/savanna mosaic produced by cultivation, into a succession of savanna woodlands, which become savanna grasslands as the desert areas are approached. The vast area of these grasslands supports fabulously rich resources of game in southern and eastern Africa, and encourages pastoralism there and in the Sudan belt.[2] At the extreme north and south where there are zones of Mediterranean climate, we find temperate woodlands, while the high mountain areas of both East and West Africa have their own montane vegetation.

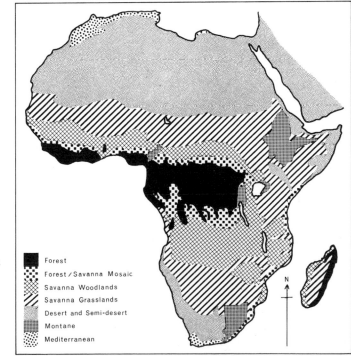

2 The Vegetation Zones of Africa.

Forest
Forest / Savanna Mosaic
Savanna Woodlands
Savanna Grasslands
Desert and Semi-desert
Montane
Mediterranean

N

This vegetation pattern, however, has not always prevailed. Overcultivation leading to erosion has changed grasslands into deserts, while slash and burn agriculture is establishing pockets of savanna in the forest fringes (the forest/savanna mosaic). In addition, there have been long-term changes in the climate. In the Ténéré, in eastern Niger, now an extremely dry desert, remains of hippopotamus bone and shells of lacustrine bivalves have been radiocarbon dated to 1400 B C ± 200 (Gif–76)[3] and 1230 B C ± 200 (Gif–284) respectively, indicating either the persistence of large lakes from earlier times or their re-formation during a recession in the desiccation of the southern Sahara. At the time of moister conditions before the beginning of the second millennium B C the Sahara was open grassland, supporting, as the rock art shows, large herds of cattle. At all times the Sahara was less of an obstacle to human movement than it has been thought to be; the trans-Saharan trade has been important for at least the last two millennia.

Before desiccation produced the desert it is likely that the forests were more extensive than they are now, probably spreading beyond the areas of forest/savanna mosaic. The study of the history of the vegetation of Africa is unfortunately still at such an early stage that we are a long way from being able to draw maps of the continent to show the vegetation at different times in the past. The identification of pollen grains left in the successive layers of soil exposed in archaeological and other excavations is of crucial importance for our understanding of the history of man in Africa. Plants are not nearly so adaptable to changes in their environment as animals are, so that pollen analysis is our primary source of evidence about changes in climate, for some plants die out and others replace them as the temperature or rainfall changes. Human history until the latest phases is very largely the story of man's interaction with his environment. In many cases his art is used in ceremonies intended to control the environment, for example, in the Bambara dance head-dresses which

Ill. 3   represent the spirit *chi wara* who in the form of an antelope introduced the knowledge of agriculture; the dances, performed in pairs by young men at the time of planting, are to ensure germination and a good harvest.

Modern Africa is populated by a great variety of peoples whose ultimate origins we seem to be further than ever from discovering. Perhaps the people who have been there longest are the Bushmen of

3 Dance headdress, in the
form of an antelope with
young, representing the spirit
chi wara who introduced agriculture to the Bambara. These
headdresses, attached to a
wickerwork cap, are worn in
pairs by young men of the
flankuru or co-operating group
of farmers who at the time of
planting and harvest dance in
imitation of a leaping antelope.
British Museum. Ht $31\frac{1}{4}$ in.

4 Ancestor figure in the Segu substyle of the Bambara. British Museum. Ht $23\frac{3}{4}$ in.

5 Face mask in the Segu substyle of the Bambara. Such masks are worn by uncircumcised boys who have a society of their own called *Ntomo*. They wear them in dances during the threshing of the millet harvest when they beg gifts of food for the society's feast; they also beat each other's legs with sticks to demonstrate their maturity by not crying out. British Museum. Ht $23\frac{1}{2}$ in.

6 Mask representing a butterfly used in invoking the deity *Do* in ceremonies asking for rain and for fertility of the fields at planting time and after the harvest. Butterflies appear in great swarms immediately after the first rains, at the beginning of the planting season, so they are an appropriate motif. Museum of Primitive Art, New York City Width 51¼ in.

the Kalahari desert, whose hunting culture appears to be very similar to that which characterized the Upper Old Stone Age. Indeed, the study of modern Bushmen has provided valuable ethnographic data for the interpretation of materials found by archaeologists.[4] Yet it seems unlikely that they still live their ancient way of life unchanged. For centuries they have been pushed by neighbouring peoples into inhospitable areas, so that their present mode of living probably reflects some readjustment to a hostile environment, rather than the life of the Old Stone Age preserved intact. The changes, however, are unlikely to have been fundamental. They never learned to work iron and have remained dependent on wood, bone and leather for the tools with which they gain their livelihood.

The Pygmies too, who occupy parts of the equatorial forest, seem to be survivors of a Stone Age population. They too hunt in the forests, though many groups have developed a symbiotic existence, exchanging the results of their hunting for agricultural produce as well as iron for their spear- and arrowheads with neighbouring Bantu farmers.

Both the Bushmen and the Pygmies are forced to migrate extensively in their pursuit of game. Their homes are, therefore, the simplest of shelters – a few branches or saplings, which the Pygmies in their moister environment thatch with leaves. This gives little scope for the development of architecture, or even for decoration of their homes (in contrast to the Indians of the American plains who were also migratory hunters but whose *tipi*, made of buffalo skins, was carried round with them and became a support for drawings and paintings). Similarly the Bushmen and Pygmies have very few material possessions to hamper their movement from place to place, though these may well be decorated, as in the case of ostrich egg shells used by the Bushmen as water-containers. Because of their way of life the plastic arts are not practised by these peoples, yet this does not mean that their life is devoid of art. Music and dancing are highly developed in both societies.[5]

Ill. 7

The Bushmen, however (like the hunting peoples of Australia), have practised glyptic art on natural features – engravings and paintings on natural outcrops of rock or on cave walls. The places where these arts were practised seem to have been the centres to which these hunters returned time after time, assembling in large groups for ceremonies such as the initiation of the young men and marriages between bands. This regular return to a centre for the performance of ceremonies on behalf of the community may well be the basic need which eventually led, when a regular supply of food could be assured by agriculture, to permanent settlement and ultimately to the growth of towns. While the ephemeral arts, music, dance, poetry and narration can be practised anywhere no matter how small the group, the enduring arts of painting and sculpture depend largely on having permanent settlements, i.e. on an agriculturally based society, or at least on the possession of a ritual focal point to which the migratory groups can return from time to time.

Many of the peoples of Africa lead a pastoral existence, herding cattle or sheep and goats. They too lead a largely migratory life, seeking fresh pastures or water for themselves and their herds. In general their opportunity for expression in the enduring arts is limited but they do frequently decorate their milking-vessels and some have developed the art of basketwork to a high level, since

16

7 Decorated ostrich egg-
shell drinking-vessel used
by Bushmen at Luderitz
Bay, Nabib desert, South-
West Africa. The engraved
lines are filled with red and
black pigment. Ethno-
logical Collection of the
University of Zürich.
Ht 5⅞ in.

baskets are easily transported being both light in weight and not
easily broken. Nevertheless pastoralists too when the opportunity
presents itself express themselves through painting. The Masai of
Kenya and northern Tanganyika not only paint their shields with
decorations which indicate their group or section, but they occasionally paint these and other motifs on immobile surfaces such as rock
shelters and even concrete cisterns.[6] One of the richest treasures of
African art, the Saharan rock paintings, was bequeathed to us by
pastoral peoples, who evidently returned time and time again to the
same locations which provided temporary foci for their society,
probably when their youths were initiated, for it is this regularly
recurring ceremony which serves to give cohesion not only to mi-
grant societies, but also to groups of agriculturists living in scattered
settlements without towns or strong centralized political institutions.
Among such groups initiation is often the main institution which
expresses their unity and which also demands the supply of art
objects such as masks and head-dresses for use in the ceremonies.

In the main, however, it is the settled agriculturists who have produced most of the well-known sculpture of Africa, especially those of the rain forest who grow predominantly root crops, and some of the cereal cultivators of the savanna woodlands which fringe the forests. Outside this area, among the mixed farmers and herdsmen of eastern and southern Africa, sculpture is usually small in scale and not highly developed.[7] The people who occupy the core area of African sculpture are not all of one group – not only are there the so-called 'true forest Negro', but also palaeonigritic peoples (of small stature, living in refuge areas where they seem to have been driven by later immigrants) and Bantu-speaking peoples. The predominance of this area is probably due to the coincidence of two important factors. One is the agricultural basis of the community, which permitted permanent settlements where major works of sculpture could be safely preserved and architecture developed which in turn called for sculptors to produce doors, shutters and houseposts; the other factor is the availability of timber in varieties to suit all purposes – heavy durable woods like *iroko* (*Chlorophora excelsa*) for houseposts, lighter ones like *Cordia Millenii* for drums and dance masks. Where sculpture occurs in the lighter woodlands of eastern and southern Africa, its scale is reduced and clay or beadwork constructions are often used. An examination of the wooden figures in Holy, 1967, shows that only the four tomb pillars from Ethiopia, which range from 120 to 133 centimetres, exceed a height of ninety-five centimetres, the median height for the whole group being fifty-three centimetres[8], while the masks range from eight to seventy-five centimetres with a median of twenty-six centimetres. In contrast, the series taken from 122 different traditions across the whole continent in William Fagg, 1965, show a range in size of figures from 17·5 to 120 centimetres (with a single example 175 centimetres tall) and a median size of sixty-one centimetres, while the masks range from twenty-two to 105 centimetres (with a single outlier 172 centimetres long) and a median size of forty centimetres. It appears then, and this hardly needs to be demonstrated, that the lack of generously sized timber had an inhibiting effect on large-scale wood carvings, but the effect is greater than that. The availability of materials, often coupled with elaborate political institutions, seems to have encouraged artistic production in quantity, and in Africa, as elsewhere, quality seems to be in part dependent on this. It is the most productive traditions which

8, 9 The production of figure sculpture does not, of course, preclude an interest in decorative arts. The BaKuba excel in both fields. These are examples of their raffia pile cloth. Hampton Institute, Hampton, Virginia.

10 Many African peoples who do not produce figure sculpture carve and decorate their everyday objects most beautifully. This is a wooden stool, inlaid with copper and brass wire, used by elders among the AKamba. Manchester Museum. Diameter 9 in.

11 Similarly, the MaShona are best known for their decorative headrests, used like a pillow to protect their elaborate hair-styles. This one was collected at Umtali, Southern Rhodesia. Manchester Museum. Ht $4\frac{3}{8}$ in.

12 Plastic art among the Lozi (formerly better known as the BaRotse) is best represented in museum collections by basketwork in their characteristic technique. They do, however, perform dances which employ masks constructed of bark cloth over a wickerwork frame, as well as others carved of wood. British Museum. L. $24\frac{1}{2}$ in.

13 (*left*) Figure sculptures outside the main area of distribution seem to have been produced by peoples who have migrated from the forests and woodlands. This piece is a Zulu work, but nothing is known of its use. British Museum. Ht 24¾ in.

14 (*above*) The MaKonde, who produced this mask for use by their men's society, are a group who have migrated from the southern Congo Basin towards the east coast of the continent. Artistically they are to be related to the BaLuba style complex (*Ills. 218–222*). British Museum. Ht 10 in.

have given us some of the finest African sculpture for high productivity indicates sufficient commissions not only to keep the gifted carver in practice but to enable him to develop his style. To be sure it also means that there will be work for less able carvers too. Father Carroll's remarks on this are highly pertinent, for he has had many years of close contact with carvers working in what is probably the richest tradition, that of the Yoruba:

'Constant, suitable work is necessary for the full development of a carver's abilities. It was the group of carvers in a district – repeating the same themes and only gradually introducing new ones – which

15, 16 Bowl in the form of a kneeling woman, carved in Ilesha, where it was captured by Ibadan soldiers during the 1880s after which time it was kept in the Compound of the Olubadan, until he sold it in 1953. Coll. R. P. Armstrong. Ht 11½ in.

built up a cumulative genius capable of supporting the less gifted carvers. It was . . . this evolution as a group, rather than the religious intensity or emotion of the carvers, which gave much of its artistic power to the old carving. If sufficient carvers could be similarly employed – and fully employed – in modern conditions, the artistic level of the whole group would rise and individual geniuses would emerge.'[9]

There seems to be a general coincidence of the distribution of wood sculpture in Africa with the distribution of the forests and woodlands. It seems likely that the area where the earliest settled agricultural communities had generous supplies of wood available to them was on the edges of the forest in West Africa. Precisely when and where is still obscure but the oldest sculpture we know so far from south of the Sahara comes from this very area – the terracotta sculptures of the Nok culture of Nigeria which date from at least the second half of the first millennium B C and have indications of a wood-carving tradition preceding them, for some of the sculptures are in a subtractive style characteristic of wood carving, in which pieces are removed from the mass to produce the sculpture, whereas plastic

17 *Nimba* mask used in rituals of the *Simo* Society of the northern Baga after the rice harvest. These magnificent sculptures of imposing size are worn over the head and resting on the shoulders of the dancer who usually sees out through a slot between the breasts of the figure. British Museum. Ht (without the fibre costume) 48 in.

18 Drum from the Southern Baga, whose style is very different from that of the Northern Baga seen in the *nimba* mask, in *Ill. 17*. This type of drum has been said to be used in funeral ceremonies of members of the *Simo* Society, but this is unlikely to be its only use. British Museum. Ht 44 in.

media like terracotta are normally in an additive style, being built up by applying more material.

These few remarks about the influence of the environment and the way of life upon the potential capacity of the people to produce sculpture or painting are about as much as can safely be said by way of generalization. However, the art of the forest and the art of the savanna are often contrasted, and the differences related to the characteristics of the societies in these varying environments. It has been claimed, for example, that the peoples of the forest do not form large social groups; that they live in isolated communities, in fear of the forest and of each other; that the continuous fight to keep their clearings from being encroached upon by the forest absorbs all their energy and depresses their spirits. In contrast, the peoples of the savanna built up empires (ancient Ghana, Songhay, the Northern Nigerian Emirates) with a state organization, a large and specialized administrative machinery, a governing class to patronize the artist, and public feasts and ceremonies to utilize his products.[10] This is very much a theoretical picture expressing how a European might expect an African to react to his environment, rather than one based on observed facts. (It reflects too the admiration felt by some administrators of the former Colonial powers for the peoples and cultures of Muslim Africa, who were felt to be already civilized, and the relative contempt for those who retained their own religious beliefs and way of life, who were regarded as barbarians if not as savages.) Anthropologists and other social scientists who have approached African peoples with more open minds have shown how mistaken this logical model is. Colin Turnbull has most eloquently described the life of the Pygmies of the Ituri Forest in Congo-Kinshasa, showing that they are among the most happily disposed people in the world, who look upon the forest as a friendly provider of their food.[11] Moreover, some of the most powerful states of Africa arose in the forests: Benin, Ijebu and Ife for example. In any case the Sudanese states were not as centralized as European scholars have imagined. There was no fixed capital city for example, and administration operated through family and village heads whose authority came from their role in the ancestor cult and from their connection with the land. Many of these empires were based on Islam, which, officially at least, discouraged rather than encouraged representational art, though this did in fact continue as a means of serving the ancestors rather than the court.

Ills. 3–5
Ills. 17–18

On the other hand Griaule points out that 'the Bambara, the Kurumba and the Baga' – all savanna peoples – 'have certainly not founded states. But they have created certain institutions, like that of initiation which can develop . . . an accumulation of material; in the life of art they play the role of a state by establishing rules which extend beyond narrowing horizons and remain applicable with some variations, to the larger districts.'[12] This is a much more valuable idea and one thinks immediately of the *Poro* Society, best documented from Liberia[13] but influential also in Sierra Leone (from where indeed the name *Poro* comes), Guinea and the Ivory Coast. Masks used in
Ills. 174–175 its rites abound in museum collections.

CHAPTER TWO

The Development of the Study of African Art

The greatest contribution Africa has made so far to the cultural heritage of mankind is its richly varied sculpture. African sculpture was scarcely known outside its own continent until late in the nineteenth century, but during the present century its liberating and refreshing effect on Western art has been immeasurable. African sculpture is a highly developed and extremely sophisticated art form with thousands of years of history behind it, yet it is still sometimes discussed as a subdivision of 'primitive art', a concept which derives from Darwinian evolution. There was a theory, derived from Leonardo da Vinci, that painting was the highest form of art and the latest to evolve. It followed that societies which possessed only sculpture were backward. The discovery of Old Stone Age cave paintings in the late nineteenth century destroyed this as a theory, but the idea of backward, unevolved, 'primitive' art continued.

The word 'primitive' of course is Protean in its meanings. Its basic sense is 'primary in time', and by extension undeveloped, simple, crude, unsophisticated. But so-called 'primitive' art is none of these things, and indeed the oldest art we know, the most primitive in its strictest time sense – the Old Stone Age cave paintings of Europe – is highly sophisticated. All art is sophisticated; if it were not sophisticated it would not be art, but merely a felicitous accident.

An attempt is sometimes made among art historians to justify the use of the term 'primitive art' on the grounds that 'we know what we mean by it' and that the various traditions share in common a disrespect for naturalism in the proportions of the human body. Art historians may think that they know what they mean by the term, though they have failed to produce a working definition; if we accept the disrespect for naturalistic proportions as symptomatic, then a great deal of twentieth-century Western art should be embraced under the term 'primitive art', while the rest of the art of the Western world could with equal justice be lumped together as 'the art of social realism'. Moreover, art historians also speak of the 'Italian primitives' who are in a certain sense 'primary in time', and of the primitivism of certain modern painters when they refer to the naivety of their vision. Even as used by art historians the term has several distinct meanings.

The term 'primitive art' is a legacy from the anthropologists of the nineteenth century who saw the Europe of their day as the apex of social evolution. As it is currently used it is a negative, not a positive concept – it has to be defined as the art of the areas outside the Western and Oriental traditions. (If there had not been written sources about Oriental art, it too might have been considered 'primitive'.) Surely this is an ethnocentric definition. The only sensible way to approach foreign art traditions is on their own terms, and so as not to prejudge them we should speak of them by their regions of origin as traditional African, Oceanic or American art. We must say 'traditional' for in all these areas of the world the old art forms are changing or have changed and the artists are being drawn into the cosmopolitan world of twentieth-century art, as we shall see in the concluding chapter.[14]

African art is usually considered to consist exclusively of sculpture and to have no recoverable history. In fact, the earliest art we know from Africa is glyptic, not plastic – paintings and engravings on exposures of smooth stone – and although by the beginning of the present century painting seems to have become much less important than sculpture, the most exciting developments in contemporary African art are in painting rather than sculpture. Moreover, archaeological investigations are being conducted in many parts of Africa, and we are learning more and more about the history of African sculpture, so far chiefly in Nigeria. It is still too soon to write a history of African art, but we shall look at some of the sources which will contribute to such a history when eventually it comes to be written.

In order to understand how ideas on the subject of African art have changed with time and with increased knowledge, we must refer to a number of studies which did not draw exclusively on African material, and even to some which did not discuss it at all.

Serious study of African, American, and Oceanic art began in the second half of the nineteenth century, a period when the idea of

19 Three figures from the Lobi, probably from an ancestor shrine. The large one appears to be called *kontornbe*, the small ones *kô pwimda*. British Museum. Hts 17½, 28½ and 14¾ in.

evolution was permeating all scientific thought. In consequence, the study of the arts of these little-known areas was directed towards seeking out the ultimate origin of art, through studies of decoration of surfaces rather than through sculpture. Many of those involved saw themselves as anthropologists, rather than as art historians, and saw the art they studied as a reflection of progress in the material culture of mankind as a whole. The first discovery of the Stone Age cave paintings of Europe was made at Altamira in 1878 but it was not until the first decade of the twentieth century that their antiquity was generally accepted. Before these discoveries, would-be students of the origins and evolution of art had to proceed by inference and deduction from modern examples. One of the first writers was Gottfried Semper, whose book *Style in the technical and tectonic Arts, or practical Aesthetics* appeared in the early 1860s.[15] Semper, an architect, was primarily concerned with the study of architectural forms. His argument was that since man's first need was for protection for himself and his fire, he plaited grass mats to keep out the wind and rain. The technique of plaiting produced a pattern which led to the development of weaving techniques and the deliberate seeking after pattern. Later, when the making of pottery began, basketwork designs were copied on to it, the difference of material leading to

20 Wooden figure representing a member of the Lilwa Society who was hanged for revealing its secrets, and intended to remind initiates of the importance of secrecy. BaMbole. Musée Royale de l'Afrique Centrale, Tervuren. Ht $36\frac{1}{4}$ in.

modifications in the patterns. This line of argument was built up by his followers into a deterministic, materialistic system for the explanation of all non-Western art forms. The real weakness, of course, is that Semper had no facts to support his hypothesis, which was constructed by extrapolation from his own thoughts. However, it stimulated other workers to look for the appropriate data and W. H. Holmes wrote a number of articles between 1883 and 1903 contributing to the theory.[16] Then Max Schmidt published his *Indian Studies in Central Brazil* in 1905.[17] He showed how motifs developed from plaiting techniques were applied in pottery decoration but he clearly selected his data to fit the hypothesis, rather than constructing the hypothesis to fit the data. He ignored, for example, such motifs as spirals and wavy lines which although geometric are difficult to derive from straight-line plaiting. Moreover, as Adrian Gerbrands points out, Schmidt ignored the fact that the Australian aborigines have rectilinear and curvilinear designs but no basketwork of the type from which such designs are supposed to be exclusively derived.[18]

Realism in art was explained in accordance with this theory by the assumption that a geometric design reminded someone of a natural object, which led to a deliberate attempt to increase the realism of the representation. This entire theory, of course, is strongly evolutionary in character and it was opposed by a school of thought which was no less evolutionary in its thinking, but which had the merit of beginning with the data and building its hypothesis round them. The hypothesis is known as the 'degeneration theory', for its proponents demonstrated that slavish copying of a naturalistic representation without understanding led to purely geometric forms. The principal contributions to these studies came from Hjalmar Stolpe[19], A.C. Haddon[20], A.H. Lane-Fox Pitt-Rivers[21] and Henry Balfour[22]; the last was later the curator of the museum which Oxford University built to house the Pitt-Rivers Collection of artefacts from all over the world, and intended to demonstrate evolution in all classes of man-made objects, not just in art. The material studied was all contemporary, an objection which the degeneration school was quick to recognize so the 'older' types were called 'survivals'. On the whole their work was quite self-critical and still makes interesting reading, but their data had to be collected from whatever sources were available, and were often of dubious value. The whole argument rested on inferences made from modern objects about man's earliest artistic efforts. The unproductiveness of this methodology is evident to us today, and in any case the revelation of Old Stone Age art, at about the time these men were writing, provided direct evidence of prehistoric art and its development, and superseded this hypothetical art history.

These early studies had been exclusively concerned with decoration and sought its origin only in the crafts. One, a philosophical-theoretical study by Wilhelm Worringer written in 1908[23], rejected this technological basis for the origin of art. He saw all art as basically the expression of volition, though this might be modified by purpose, raw material and other technical considerations. He affords valuable insights: 'what appears from our standpoint the greatest distortion must have been at the time, for its creator, the highest beauty and the fulfilment of his artistic volition'.[24] Indeed, his insights into the nature of abstraction in art made his study one of the most durable influences in the gradual acceptance of modern art in Europe, as is reflected by the fact that it was still considered worth translating into English as late as in 1953. Yet Worringer was a thoroughgoing evolutionist, who believed the earliest forms of art to have been geometric abstractions which led logically and inevitably to naturalism so that he rejected the representational cave paintings of southern France as not being art at all, because his theory could not embrace them. Similarly he repudiated 'the "artistic achievements" of African natives' and of 'the majority of primitive peoples'[25], excepting only those who have exercised their artistic gifts in a purely ornamental field.

The study of ornament went in a new direction under the lead of Franz Boas, who was to become one of the most influential teachers in America in the field of anthropology. His first major work was a study of 'The Decorative Art of the Indians of the North Pacific Coast of America', published in 1897[26] and revised and reprinted in his *Primitive Art* (1927), which is still kept in print; it has had a remarkably long life for a single paper. The rest of this later book draws on work carried out under his direction by his pupils Dixon, Kroeber, Lowie and Wissler in surveying the meaning of ornamental designs among North American Indians. In this book, Boas demolished the degeneration theory though, since the American Indian art dealt with by the survey was largely ornamental, his ideas refer more to ornament than to sculpture. Boas considered that art could not exist until the artist had developed sufficient skill to dominate his material; this is true enough but does not have much practical application. He also pointed out that although form, symmetry and rhythm together have an aesthetic effect in themselves, form can also convey meaning, which adds an emotional value to the form, increasing its effect. Boas divides art into two categories – representative (nowadays more commonly known as 'representational') art and symbolism (which had previously been known as 'geometric' art). In the former category form and content are about equally important, but in symbolic art the content is much more important than the form. Having made this useful distinction Boas went on to concentrate on symbolic art and its meaning, almost as if it were the whole of art. Nevertheless, one conclusion to which these studies led him is vital for all kinds of art – that the same form can convey different meanings in different societies. It follows of course that form and content cannot be considered separately in studies of development through time, of distribution in space, or in the combination of both these aspects, which we call 'diffusion'. Boas himself did not seem to realize this for he regarded the form as basic and of technical origin, and the meaning as a secondary accretion

21 This figure was collected by Northcote Thomas at Sabongida, forty-five miles north-east of Benin in Afenmai Division, Nigeria. Its cubistic qualities reflect the artistic tradition of the Edo-speaking peoples of the Benin Empire which contrasts with the better-known art of the Benin court. (*Ills. 84–88, 97, 169–71, 251.*) Cambridge University Museum of Archaeology and Ethnology. Ht $24\frac{1}{4}$ in.

Another classic, of broader scope than those already mentioned, for it puts the problems of art and decoration in the wider setting of material culture as a whole, is R. U. Sayce's *Primitive Arts and Crafts*,[27] which draws extensively and critically on earlier studies and is especially valuable for its cautionary examples, particularly of the convergence of designs from totally different sources.

One lesson from these early studies is still important; it is perfectly true that weaving techniques, whether in matting, basketry or cloth, tend by their very nature to produce a series of motifs of essentially geometric character, which we might call 'technomorphs' since their form arises from the technique. Any society possessing any of these weaving techniques is likely also to have the corresponding technomorphs which may be copied in other media, e.g. plaitwork designs are found on Benin pottery and wood and ivory carvings. Since there is a strong possibility that these motifs had an independent origin within the society they are unsuitable for use as indicators of the influence of one society upon another.

Two-dimensional design has been rather neglected of late in favour of sculpture, but one recent book on *African Design*, by Margaret Trowell[28] deserves to be mentioned. This is a far more sophisticated and much less pretentious study than its forerunners. It describes the materials and the varieties of designs employed throughout Africa. The author freely admits that it is but a sampling of the immensely rich material which is available, and the only flaw is that the selection is so heavily weighted with East African material that some of the judgments made do not always apply to West Africa.

The study of sculpture, as opposed to ornament, began in the last years of the nineteenth century and most of the literature follows one or the other of two approaches: the ethnological one, which is essentially similar to Boas' in considering a knowledge of the content of a work of art to be essential to its understanding and even for its appreciation; and the aesthetic one, which considers that such knowledge is unnecessary for its appreciation. In the extreme form of this second approach, exemplified by Carl Einstein's *Negerplastik*,[29] such knowledge was indeed held to interfere with the aesthetic enjoyment of the work of art.

These two schools of thought have gradually approached each other, for anthropologists are paying increasing attention to aesthetics and art history, and art critics are paying increasing attention to the cultural background of African art – for, after all, form and content are scarcely separable in societies in which the artist is an integral member of the community, not an individual struggling to express a purely private vision.

At first anthropologists treated sculpture simply as an aspect of religion, but soon took note of the divergence from natural proportions shown in the sculptures. This was commonly regarded as a child-like trait – a shift of emphasis resulting only from over-attention to details at the expense of the overall form. Field studies of artists at work eventually showed that great care is taken in blocking out the form of the sculpture, so the proportions are set from the beginning and the detailed work left to the end.[30]

One of the first anthropologists to make Africa his special field of study was Leo Frobenius. As early as 1896 he was writing about the art of non-European peoples, suggesting that they have an impulse to copy natural forms and that these copies convey ideas and meaning – i.e. the content gives significance to the form. Faithful copying from nature thus becomes, after a while, less necessary, provided that the form evokes sufficient associations to convey the meaning. Such reactions are, of course, culturally determined, so the form has this meaning only for the society to which it belongs.[31] Frobenius unfortunately did not pursue this valuable idea, but went on later to theorize that sculpture with large heads had originated from a practice of placing the skull on a stick over the grave – a quite unprovable hypothesis. Similarly, he saw the mask as originating in the practice – common in the Pacific – of preserving the skull of an ancestor in a little grass hut, but this is too broad and comprehensive a theory to carry conviction.[32]

Before Frobenius began to write Gauguin had gone to Tahiti, the most extravagant individual act of turning to a non-European culture in the decades immediately before and after 1900, when European artists were avid for new artistic experiences, but it was only about 1904–5 that African art began to make its distinctive impact. One piece is still identifiable; it is a mask that had been given to *Ill. 22* Maurice Vlaminck in 1905. He records that Derain was 'speechless' and 'stunned' when he saw it, bought it from Vlaminck and in turn showed it to Picasso and Matisse, who were also greatly affected by it. Ambroise Vollard then borrowed it and had it cast in bronze by

Maillol's bronzesmith. The revolution of twentieth-century art was under way.

Many artists have recorded their reactions on first encountering African art. Georges Braque recalled that 'les masques nègres . . . m'ont ouvert un horizon nouveau'.★ Juan Gris even made a cardboard *Ill. 183* copy of a funerary figure from Gabon to decorate his apartment in 1922. This is an avenue of great interest, which unfortunately cannot be pursued here. The reader is recommended to read Michel Leiris's account (1968) for he knew many of these artists personally, and that of Jean Laude (1968) and to see the works which European artists collected illustrated in the Musée de l'Homme catalogue: *Arts Primitifs dans les Ateliers d'Artistes* (Paris, 1967).[33]

The first works which these artists saw were of no more than average quality but their interest led others, not only practising artists, to a heightened sensitivity to African sculpture. This increasing interest, however, encouraged a flow of writings characterized in general more by enthusiasm than by understanding. An essentially subjective approach – that which asks no more than 'what does this sculpture mean to me?' – is valid enough in judging any artist's work, but, of course, does not lead to the fullest possible understanding of an art for which some knowledge of the ideas of the society in which the artist practised is vital.

One of the first to attempt to set the art in its social and cultural background was E. Vatter, *Religiöse Plastik der Naturvölker* (Religious Sculpture of Primitive Peoples) (Frankfurt, 1926). He pointed out that the artist's role is not, as it has generally been in modern Europe, to express his own personality, but rather to serve the community. He goes on to assert that the African artist is anonymous, an idea which was unquestioningly accepted, and probably responsible for the fact that for a long time no one bothered to ask the names of artists. As will become clear later, not only is the individual artist known in a great many African societies, but the better the artist, the more widespread is his fame.

In the 1920s another German, Eckart von Sydow, was at work, and produced five books which approached the art of Africa and Oceania from a number of different points of view, including that of psychoanalysis, though he began as an art historian. In 1930 there

★ 'Negro masks . . . opened a new horizon for me.'

36

22 Mask made by the Fang, given in 1905 to Maurice Vlaminck who sold it to André Derain. It was seen also by Picasso and Matisse. This was not the first African sculpture to attract Vlaminck, but it appears to be the only one from this time which is still certainly identifiable. Coll. Alice Derain. Ht $18\frac{7}{8}$ in.

appeared his *Handbuch der Afrikanischen Plastik, I Die Westafrikanische Plastik* (Handbook of African sculpture, West African sculpture) (Berlin) which incorporated documentation from museums and from the literature. This is a monument of thorough compilation and is of lasting value as a source. The second part, *Afrikanische Plastik* (African sculpture) was published posthumously in 1954 (ed. G. Kutscher, Berlin). In the course of this work von Sydow came to realize that only field-work could produce adequate documentation, so in 1936 he visited Nigeria, but his book about this trip, *Im Reiche der Gottähnlicher Herrscher* (In the Kingdoms of the Divine Rulers) (Brunswick), entertaining as it is, is no more than a travelogue.

At the same time, others were working on museum collections, and this led to the still classic studies of C. Kjersmeier, *Centres de Style de la Sculpture Nègre Africaine* (Centres of Style of African Negro Sculpture), in four volumes (Paris and Copenhagen 1935–38);

37

23 Houseposts carved by a Yoruba sculptor in Ketu, Dahomey and sent as a present from the Alaketu to the Oni of Ife in 1938. The interlace designs and the choice of colours are characteristic of Yoruba sculpture in Dahomey. Ife Museum. Ht Left: 58 in. Right: 60 in.

24 Like the houseposts, carved doors may be used in shrines or simply to decorate the house of an important man. This one was collected in Modakeke, Ife. Ife Museum. $50\frac{1}{2} \times 23$ in.

F. M. Olbrechts, *Plastiek van Kongo* (Antwerp 1946);[34] and P. S. Wingert, *The Sculpture of Negro Africa* (New York 1950).

Yet a different approach was being made by two of Boas's pupils, Melville Herskovits and F. M. Olbrechts. Herskovits had worked in Dahomey in 1931 investigating all aspects of Fon culture. He encouraged his students to do field-work, and three of them have contributed to our knowledge of art and artists in Africa: W. R. Bascom, Justine Cordwell and James Fernandez. Similarly, Olbrechts encouraged his pupils A. Maesen, P. J. L. Vandenhoute and D. Biebuyck to work in the field. Marcel Griaule led expeditions from the Sorbonne to the Dogon in 1931, 1935 and 1937, and his pupils who accompanied him dispersed to work elsewhere in Africa – Germaine Dieterlen, Solange de Ganay, J. P. Lebeuf and Denise Paulme among others. Independently F. H. Lem did field-work in the western Sudan.[35] This book owes a great deal to the studies carried out by these observers, and also by Hans Himmelheber (working in the field in 1933 and later) and his son E. Fischer, as will be apparent later.

In the English-speaking world, however, the principal contributor to the study of African art is William Fagg, who began by studying the well-documented collections of the British Museum before making visits to Africa for study in the field in 1949–50, 1953, and 1958–59, as well as frequent shorter visits more recently. He has worked especially in Nigeria where his brother, Bernard Fagg, Government archaeologist and later Director of Antiquities, discovered the prehistoric sculptures of the Nok culture, the oldest African sculpture we know outside of Egypt. William Fagg's books *The Sculpture of Africa* (with Eliot Elisofon) (London 1958); *Nigerian Images* (London, 1963); and *Tribes and Forms in African Art* (Paris, 1966) as well as numerous exhibition catalogues are characterized by the accuracy of their documentation of individual pieces.

Fagg's work in Nigeria owed a debt to that of Kenneth Murray, the first head of the Department of Antiquities, the results of whose researches are mostly to be found in the documentation of the Nigerian Museum in Lagos. An artist himself, Murray worked closely with practising artists and cult groups long before he was asked to undertake in 1943 a survey of Nigerian antiquities, which not only led to the establishment of the Department but revealed that Nigeria was even richer in sculptural traditions than the Congo Basin.

Work in the field in Africa is now almost a *sine qua non*, and very few writers' views on African art are taken seriously unless they are rooted in a field study. Increasingly, the really valuable writings on African art consist of detailed studies of limited areas. Some books do, however, draw carefully and critically on the literature based on field-work. The outstanding example of this is Adrian Gerbrands's *Art as an Element of Culture, especially in Negro Africa* (Leiden, 1957), which utilizes unpublished as well as published field-work by others, and to which this book is heavily indebted.[36] Also based on a critical study of the literature and of museum collections is the book by Michel Leiris and Jacqueline Delange, *African Art* (London 1968),[37] which has an excellent introductory survey, though unfortunately the middle section of the book is organized round Marcel Mauss's tripartite division of arts of the body, arts of the surroundings and autonomous figurative arts. The attempt to discuss the whole of African art under these headings reduces the value of this section. The third part provides a very able but all too brief regional survey of art styles. The author of this section (Jacqueline Delange) has, however, published a fuller scholarly survey of the various art styles of the continent in her book *Arts et Peuples de l'Afrique Noire* (Arts and Peoples of Black Africa), (Paris, 1967). Both these books are careful to avoid those misleading generalizations about African art which I have mentioned earlier.

Margaret Trowell, however, has made generalizations about African art which are of an unusual kind.[38] She distinguishes three types of art which she calls 'spirit-regarding', 'man-regarding' and the 'art of ritual display'. This, of course, is a classificatory device for dealing with the material; it has the great merit of emphasizing the function of the art in the society which produced it, though any one society may produce sculpture which belongs in more than one category. The sculptures of the Dogon,[39] both ancestor figures and masks, are clearly directed towards influencing the world of spirits, whether of the ancestors or of the animals and trees round them; similarly the sculpture of the Kalabari Ijo[40] addresses itself to the spirits rather than to man. Yet the Yoruba have masked dances, the *egungun*, which are directed both at ensuring that the ancestors will rest in peace and at entertaining the living; on the other hand their houseposts and sculptured doors on palaces and houses are *Ills. 23, 24* intended for the glorification of their owners, whereas similar carvings in shrines are for the honour of the spirits worshipped there. Without information collected in the field it would, therefore, be impossible to distinguish the secular from the religious, the man-regarding from the spirit-regarding.

Yet social scientists have to seek generalizations and anthropologists are attempting to provide a statistical basis for general statements on African art, using the techniques of the data bank. Unfortunately, the individual studies from which the initial data are drawn are of uneven quality and are often silent about certain aspects of the societies. In principle, correlations are sought between artistic characteristics and other phenomena of society whether they appear to have a direct connection or not. For example, it is obvious that one might expect to find royal ancestor figures only in societies which had a king (for these are not entirely independent variables). Alvin Wolfe's statistical examination of the 'Social Structural Bases of Art'[41] confirms the *a priori* argument on p. 16 by showing 'that both nucleation and fixity [of settlement] are somehow related to the development of art'; the correlation of art production with sodalities is only a little lower – we know that initiation societies, which often overlap traditional political boundaries are among the principal patrons of art in Africa. This approach is in its infancy and so far relatively elementary questions are being asked – Wolfe's study is concerned principally with the amount of art produced, based on the estimates of eighteen other scholars – but it points the way to further investigation.[42]

Progress is, however, handicapped by the relatively small numbers of detailed studies of African sculpture in the field and this is a matter of great urgency, for the traditional cultural bases of the art are being supplanted daily. Fortunately, anthropologists already orientated towards field-work by their discipline are becoming increasingly aware of the importance of art in African societies, while art historians are not only turning more and more to Africa as a field of study but also undertaking studies in the field which, superficially at least, are difficult to distinguish from those of anthropologists. Recently, one of the most senior figures in the study of African art complained to me that one of his younger colleagues was encouraging his students to be anthropologists rather than art historians. Surely if we are to understand African art we need to draw on both these disciplines.

42

CHAPTER THREE

Towards a History of African Art

DRAWINGS AND PAINTINGS ON ROCK

African art has often been written about as if it were static and always the same, but it has in fact been continuously evolving, although the rate of change has varied from time to time and from place to place. Radiocarbon dates coupled with oral traditions suggest that the intensely naturalistic style of sculpture at Ife lasted about the same length of time as bronze-casting has lasted in Benin; yet the Ife work, although it is richly varied, because of the individual styles of the several sculptors involved, shows an essentially unaltered canon from the tenth to the fourteenth centuries, whereas at Benin from the fifteenth to the nineteenth centuries the progression from a moderate naturalism to a considerable degree of stylization can be demonstrated.[43]

Evidence of the history of African art is available from a variety of sources, which are naturally of uneven value, but we have certainly come a long way since 1950, when Griaule could write: 'We shall not speak of prehistoric art of which numerous rupestral examples have been preserved, nor of historical art where the data are non-existent.'[44]

The main contribution to our knowledge of the history of African art has come from archaeological explorations. Since Griaule wrote many more examples of painting and engraving on rocks have come to light in many parts of Africa and many discoveries of ancient sculpture have been made. Oddly enough, African rock paintings and engravings were discovered earlier than the European ones.

Paintings of animals had been reported in Mozambique as early as 1721, and the first mention was made of Bushman paintings in South Africa in 1752,[45] whereas the European ones were totally unknown

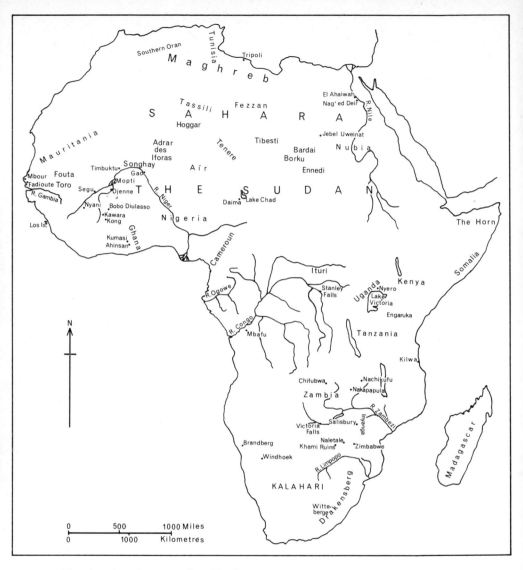

25 Map showing places mentioned in the text.

44

until de Sautuola's daughter looked up at the roof of the cave of Altamira in 1878. The engravings of North Africa were first discovered by a group of French Army officers travelling in southern Oran in 1847; they reported engravings of elephants, lions, antelopes, bovids, ostriches, gazelles and human beings armed with bows and arrows. When the great explorer Heinrich Barth crossed the Sahara from Tripoli to Timbuktu in 1850, he found similar engravings in the Fezzan. Discoveries have continued to accumulate, so that it is now clear that all the mountainous regions of the Sahara contain rock engravings and paintings. Over thirty thousand examples are known, half of them in the Tassili.[46]

They are not all of the same age and various criteria have been employed in attempting to date them, both relatively and absolutely. Relative dating is, of course, more easily achieved than absolute dating, for several types of evidence can help to indicate succession in any given series of engravings or paintings. Styles change with time and sometimes a drawing in one style overlaps and is therefore later than the

26 Engraving of an elephant at Bardai in the eastern Sahara, of either the *Bubalus* or the Cattle Period. Ht 7 to 8 in.

27 Faceless (aniconic) figure at Tin Teferiest, Tassili. Archaic Period. Smaller figures in a related style appear to be superimposed on it, but Lajoux says it is impossible to determine which was painted first. The difficulty of establishing such relationships complicates the establishment of the stylistic sequence in all studies of rock art. Ht 39 in.

28 Stone figure at Eshure, Ekiti, North-eastern Yorubaland. The trunk is covered with spiral-headed iron nails similar to those found on stone sculptures at Ife, to which the group of sculptures at Eshure is probably related. It is unlikely that these are later than the fourteenth century AD and probable that they are several centuries older. Ht 42 in.

underlying style. The subject-matter reflects change too: some Saharan rock engravings represent animals now extinct in the area: elephant, rhinoceros, hippopotamus and the buffalo known as *Bubalus antiquus*. Pictures of domestic cattle are younger, and more recent still are the representations of animals which are still found in the Sahara – the camel, the horse and the moufflon (a large-horned sheep). The weapons carried by the human beings also change: axes, throwing-sticks, bows, javelins, swords and finally firearms. Attempts have been made to use other criteria to indicate the relative age of engravings, such as the patination of the cut: the more closely the surface of the cut matches the weathered surface of the rock in which it is engraved, the older it is thought to be. This is not at all a reliable indication, however, for it has been demonstrated that parts of a single engraving are more heavily patinated where they have been exposed to the sun than are the parts on the shady side of the rock. Attempts have been made also to distinguish various techniques of engraving, but since no consistent correspondence has been established between these and the chronological sequence established by other evidence, it would appear that several techniques were in simultaneous use.

The rock engravings have been divided on the evidence mainly of the subject-matter, but also in part on that of their style, into four major periods, one of which is subdivided. The earliest reflects a hunting way of life, when only such wild animals as the extinct buffalo *Bubalus antiquus*, elephant, rhinoceros, hippopotamus, giraffe, large antelopes and ostriches were represented. Occasionally rams and cattle are shown, perhaps indicating a late transitional phase of the art. The animals are drawn in a naturalistic manner, often with great attention to detail: the drawings are frequently on a large scale (a rhinoceros at Wadi Djerat in the Tassili is twenty-six feet six inches long; humans are often eleven feet tall); the men are armed with clubs, throwing-sticks, axes and bows, but never with spears. This is usually called the *Bubalus Period*, and formerly 'the Hunter Period', but the drawings of rams and cattle have caused this latter term to be abandoned.

It is followed by the *Cattle (or Pastoralist) Period*. The *Bubalus antiquus* is no longer represented, but the other wild animals continue to be drawn as well as cattle. The style is rather less naturalistic; less attention is paid to details, hooves for example are often omitted; the pose is rather stiff; the horns are usually represented in 'twisted

48

perspective', i.e. frontally, when the rest of the animal is drawn in profile. The engravings are smaller in size than the earlier ones, mostly between eighteen inches and four feet in length. The men are now armed with bows.

The next, the *Horse Period*, is subdivided into three phases. The earliest is the *Chariot Sub-Period*. The elephant is occasionally represented, but not the other large pachyderms and large antelopes; domestic cattle continue, and moufflons and domesticated dogs are common. The style becomes increasingly conventionalized: the earliest chariots are well drawn, with a single shaft, and a horse on either side; later with increasing stylization the wheels and shaft alone are represented, while the human figures are reduced to two isosceles triangles set apex to apex. The engravings are still smaller: most are between ten and twenty inches. A few bows are found but new weapons are characteristic: spears and round shields, while later pictures show a dagger hanging from the forearm.

The *Horseman Sub-Period* reflects the change from horse-driving to horse-riding, though a few chariots are still represented. The same animals are drawn in a 'semi-naturalistic' style whereas the human figures continue to be schematized as two triangles. The size remains unchanged; spear, round shield and knife continue, while bows are also represented, but the choice of weapons seems to reflect local preferences in different areas. In all areas, however, the warriors wear plumed head-dresses, and Libyco-Berber written characters appear at this time in the engravings of the central Sahara.

The *Horse and Camel Sub-Period* reflects the introduction of the camel, though the horse continues in use. The same animals as before are shown, but cattle become increasingly rare. The style coarsens, though some fine semi-naturalistic drawings are still found. The drawings are of smaller size: seven to sixteen inches. The same weapons continue to be represented, as do the plumed head-dresses.

The *Camel Period* is the latest, and also the current one, for not only is the camel the principal domestic animal in the Sahara, but its owners still represent it both by engraving and by painting. The other animals shown are the present-day inhabitants of the area: antelopes, oryx, gazelles, moufflons, ostrich, humped cattle (zebu) and goats. The horse is still occasionally found, especially in Mauritania, fitted with an Arab type of saddle with stirrups. The style is highly schematic; the double triangle form of human figure gives way to even simpler linear forms, and the drawings are smaller than ever, a mere six to eight inches. At first the spear is the only weapon shown, but it is later supplemented by the sword and firearms.

This general scheme of development serves as a basic guide in studying the paintings, most of which were found after this scheme was constructed. A more detailed framework, however, will be required to relate together the more numerous styles of paintings which can be distinguished.

Paintings are less widely distributed than engravings, for they need smooth surfaces, and to survive at all they must be sheltered from the elements. Paintings so protected have been found on the Ennedi Plateau, the Jebel Uweinat, the Hoggar, Tibesti, parts of Mauritania, but most spectacularly in the Tassili. Until Henri Lhote's expedition to the Tassili in 1956–57, most of the paintings had appeared to fit into the same categories as the engravings. The immense numbers of paintings revealed there by this and succeeding expeditions have forced some reassessment. The Tassili paintings surpass in numbers, in artistic quality and in variety of styles all the previously known paintings. At least thirty styles have now been distinguished, many of which can be grouped within the three major divisions of cattle, horse, and camel; of the remainder, though some may be contemporary with the *Bubalus* Period, the majority seem to be intermediate between this and the Cattle (or Pastoralist) Period. In this, sometimes known as the *Archaic Period*, there was considerable use of symbols, and also masks are represented which appear to resemble West African ones of the present time. It has been suggested that this style represents the earliest known art by black Africans. It is interesting that at first the head is featureless, as it is for example on a stone *Ills. 27–29* sculpture from Eshure in Yorubaland in Nigeria; the masked figures are later.

Stone implements abound all over the Sahara – the detailed distribution map suggests that whenever a traveller has been forced to halt his progress and descend from his vehicle to attend to a call of nature, he has discovered archaeological artefacts. The whole area appears to have been populated in the past, with a sequence of cultures from the relatively uncommon pebble tools of the earliest Old Stone Age, through abundant examples of the hand-axes of the Chelles-Acheul complex, apparently made by a variety of Pithecanthropus called *Atlanthropus mauritanicus* Arambourg. The Aterian complex

29 Figure of a masked dancer at Inaouanrhat, Tassili. There are paintings of such figures and of masks alone in several of the Tassili sites. It is natural to wonder whether this indicates that the painters were the ancestors of some of the mask-using peoples of the present day, though attempts to suggest specific parallels between the paintings and modern masks are not convincing. Ht *c.* 31 in.

with its tanged flint flakes (the African representative of the Levallois-Mousterian of the Middle Old Stone Age) is less abundant and has a more northerly distribution perhaps as a result of drier climatic conditions. There are no Upper Old Stone Age industries represented; apparently the Sahara was too dry for human occupation, for fossil sand-dunes have been found. There follows a sudden reoccupation by large numbers of people who made pottery, used polished stone axes and hunted with stone-tipped arrows. In the southern Sahara they often lived by fishing and hunting hippopotamus; skeletal remains suggest that they were Negroes. In some parts, cattle-raising became the mainstay of the economy. The paintings themselves give us the most information about this, for excavation in the Sahara is difficult, though not impossible, because of the lack of water, and cattle bones have been excavated from occupation deposits of the period. Gradually desiccation set in and settlements moved close to lakes and into river valleys before being finally abandoned.

How does this archaeological sequence correspond to the successive phases of the art? The major difficulty is that of demonstrating a positive connection between any one style of painting on the wall of a rock shelter and the implements or radiocarbon date from any one phase of occupation. Very few sites have been excavated; when large numbers of sites have been dug we may be able to detect regular correlations of archaeological industries with particular art styles, and by radiocarbon dating of the charcoal or bones found with the industries we may date the art styles.

At present, however, we must content ourselves with a few general indications. The earliest radiocarbon date for human occupation in the Tassili is 5450 ± 300 BC (Gif-290) from Titerast-n'-Elias no. 5 but it is not yet certain that the earliest paintings are as old as this. Hassi Meniet, in the Hoggar, just south of the Tassili, has provided a date of 3460 ± 300 BC (Sa-59) for a deposit which contained bones of the buffalo *Bubalus antiquus* and of domestic cattle. The existence side by side of the wild and domestic animals, representations of which have been taken as indicators of the different successive phases of the rock art, suggests that there was probably a transitional phase, about the time indicated by the radiocarbon dates, when wild animals were still hunted although the people owned domestic cattle.

Sites in the Tassili have produced a series of dates running from the mid-fourth to the early third millennium BC, which appear to

52

correspond to the period of the cattle paintings. The site of Titerast-n'-Elias no. 3, for example, had paintings of cattle on the walls and there were bones of cattle round the hearth which produced the date of 2610 ± 250 B C (Gif-288).[47]

These dated levels do not overlap the paintings on the walls, and so cannot be directly correlated with them. One attempt has been made to date the paint itself, from its organic content. This was a sample of whitish paint said to be 'of animal origin' covering other paintings at Initinen no. 8. The resulting radiocarbon date of 300 ± 200 B C (Gif-289) was considered to be much too young. This type of test can rarely be made since it destroys the painting itself. It will be necessary to wait until there are enough dates to handle statistically and thus allow reasonable correlations to be made with the succession of art styles.[48]

At present only a tentative outline can be drawn. The earliest human occupation of the Tassili appears to have been in the mid-sixth millennium B C, and the practice of painting seems to have begun not long afterwards. Once begun, it seems to have continued into the first millennium B C. In the Hoggar, as we have mentioned, *Bubalus antiquus* bones have been dated to the middle of the fourth millennium B C, so the *Bubalus* engravings may be supposed to have lasted as late as this. Where the round-headed figures occur alone in shelters they are reported to be associated with crude axes but never with pottery or grindstones, which are found very commonly associated with the Cattle Period paintings. The round-headed figures, therefore, may well be contemporary with the *Bubalus* series.[48a]

Ill. 27

The cattle paintings portray scenes of pastoral life, and with them are found pottery, polished stone axes, grindstones and arrowheads, as well as the bones of cattle, sheep and goats. Radiocarbon dates indicate a commencement of the period about 4000 B C; it appears to end with the arrival of horsemen, which can be dated to about 1200 B C on evidence obtained in Egypt, and also from the writings of Strabo and Herodotus, for these paintings seem to reflect Cretan influence not only in the style of the drawings (such as the flying gallop of the horses)[49] but the weapons too are Cretan. It was from Crete that the 'People of the Sea' came as allies of the Libyans of Cyrenaica to attack Egypt at this time.

In the next few centuries, the horse and war chariot carried the conquering Libyans across the greater part of the Sahara, though the

30 Camel, a small painting from the late period of Tassili art. Ouan Bender.

stylized drawings suggest that the indigenous artists never got possession of these vehicles. Increasing desiccation made life more and more difficult for horse-owners but chariots continued to be represented right up to the declining phase of engravings showing horses. The camel is the characteristic subject of the latest phase of the Saharan rock art, but the date of its introduction is still disputed. It was certainly known by Roman times, and may have been introduced about 700 B C.

Ill. 30

Painting and engraving appear to reflect, in part at least, different traditions, for not a single engraving is found on sites of the Cattle Period in the Tassili although there is plenty of suitable rock. Human beings are frequent in paintings, whereas they are rarely engraved; moreover paintings are commonly compositions of people and/or animals shown in meaningful relationships to each other, whereas the engravings almost always represent isolated subjects. It is natural to infer that these different traditions reflect differences of population. Lhote[50] suggests that the tradition of painting in the Cattle Period was introduced by pastoralists, who brought cattle to an earlier population of hunters whose art form was engraving. Yet the engravings of the *Bubalus* Period (no paintings of this period are known) are restricted to three widely separated areas – southern Oran, the Tassili and the Fezzan. Variations in the subjects represented in these three areas suggest that although the engravings may represent a common artistic tradition, they reflect different religious ideas. Lhote suggests that these engravings were made by people of white race, since an engraved plaque excavated from a Capsian layer in southern Tunisia shows a figure in a style resembling that of figures in southern Oran, and the Capsian seems to have been developed by people related to the European Crô-Magnon type.

The paintings of men with round heads Lhote considers to be later than the *Bubalus* Period engravings, and to be the work of black Africans, as also must be the paintings of the masks, which remind us in a general way of masks still used in Africa south of the Sahara. No skeletons have yet been excavated from the Tassili, though there are many graves awaiting the archaeologist.

The painters of the cattle often portray themselves in their art; with copper-coloured skin and straight hair, they look very like the cattle-herding Fulani who nowadays travel with their herds east and west from Cameroons Grasslands to Senegal. The Fulani language is now

Ill. 31

considered to have developed in the Middle Senegal Valley and the Fouta Toro,[51] and certainly the history of the people can be traced back to the eighth century A D in this area. It is tempting to assume that the nomadic pastoral Fulani painted the cattle scenes in the Tassili, but the weight of the evidence at present is not sufficient to prove this. With more detailed knowledge of the movements of people, and the mechanisms by which one language replaces another, perhaps we shall one day be able to make this assertion once again with confidence.

There is relatively little rock art in West Africa and it can best be regarded for the present as a southwards extension of the Saharan art. It was here, however, that the interesting connection was demonstrated between rock paintings, rock gongs, rock slides and initiation rites. Subsequently it was discovered that rock gongs and rock slides were widely distributed in Europe as well as Africa and that the complex might well go back into Late Stone Age times.[52]

Both engravings and paintings are found in other parts of Africa, especially in the South and the East. As in the Sahara, it appears that engraving was practised before painting, though the major periods of development of both media seem to have been contemporaneous, and indeed Willcox, 1968, has suggested that both were the work of the same people. In the southern part of the continent these art forms are commonly referred to as 'Bushman' art because we have written accounts describing Bushman painters in the late eighteenth and nineteenth centuries. For example, in 1869 Stow described the painter !Gcu-wa, who wore two or three horn paint-pots round his waist, and mentions another who had been killed some years earlier, who wore ten horn pots suspended from his belt, each containing a different colour of paint. The practice of painting seems to have died out soon afterwards, and attempts to obtain interpretations of rock paintings from Bushmen from the late nineteenth century onward have produced only relatively superficial interpretations. More recently attempts have been made to interpret the paintings in the light of recorded Bushman legends[53]: elephants have been identified as rain clouds, and the eland is seen as a moon symbol. Certainly the rarity of pictures of the springbok, the favourite quarry of the Bushmen, suggests that the art is not simply a form of hunting magic. Such interpretations, though not improbable, have sometimes been taken beyond the limits of the available evidence into the realm of fancy.

31 Herdsman and cattle at Tin Tazarift, Tassili. The lower cow wears a collar round its neck and has a forked object in its mouth. Cattle or Pastoralist Period. Figures in this series of paintings vary between 6 and 14 in. in height.

That the Bushmen made some of this art before they were forced into the inhospitable Kalahari is evident. That they made it all is less likely; indeed, some of the latest paintings and engravings seem to have been made by Bantu-speaking peoples, and some probably by Hottentots.

How far back the art goes, however, has been much disputed. It has been suggested that it is contemporary with the eastern Spanish rock paintings which it somewhat resembles in style; these are now considered to be of the very end of the Old Stone Age or of the Middle Stone Age; the material culture of their makers, however, seems to be largely derived from North Africa, although at present the surviving Spanish paintings seem to be older than the earliest North African ones. There is no direct evidence that the 'Bushman' art is as old as this; although pigments have been found buried in early occupation material in caves, it has been argued that these could have been intended for painting other things than the cave walls. Where paintings have been partly covered by the occupation material in rock shelters, the paint below the surface has usually been destroyed by the chemicals or bacteria in the soil so that an exact correlation with the archaeological deposit is ruled out. Some dating indicators have been obtained, though Willcox[54] is not prepared to accept any of them as certainly related to the cave art. The first date obtained was a radiocarbon date from charcoal associated with ochre which the Abbé Breuil claimed without any direct evidence had been used for making the paintings on the walls of Phillipp Cave in the Windhoek region of South-west Africa: 1418 ± 200 BC (C-911). More recently charcoal collected on the surface of the cave was dated AD 1670 ± 80 (R-23). The Chifubwa stream shelter in Zambia is covered with highly schematic engravings of parallel lines, of inverted U's with a line down the centre and some traces of paint: only a single stone industry, called Nachikufan I, was found in the deposit, which was covered with sterile sand which hid the engravings: the radiocarbon date was 4357 ± 250 BC (C-663). Dates for Nachikufan I at Nachikufu itself run from 5590 ± 600 BC (Y-624) up to 1510 ± 200 BC (Y-623). All the available dates for the Nachikufan complex are erratically distributed so that until we have several more dates, we cannot be sure that the Chifubwa stream shelter was decorated as early as the radiocarbon date indicated, especially as at Nakapapula, Serenje, Zambia a date of AD 770 ± 100 (Gxo-535) was obtained for a very late Nachikufan stone industry mixed with pottery in a rock shelter, the walls of which had naturalistic painting overlain by schematic motifs.[55]

Occasionally slabs of rock have cracked off the cave walls, taking part of a painting with them, and have been excavated from Late Stone Age deposits, but such sites have not yet been dated by radiocarbon. We may, however, regard it as certain that this art in southern Africa is of considerable antiquity, and that we must ignore the claim that it is all to be dated to the last two centuries.

The art and the life it depicts are essentially of a Late Stone Age type, but so was the Bushman economy itself. Although it seems probable that most of the surviving paintings were made during the last two millennia, the tradition is evidently much older. It no longer seems likely that all these manifestations of rock painting and engraving in Europe and Africa are to be considered either contemporaneous or even necessarily to represent a cultural continuum stretching from eastern Spain to the Cape; nor is there any evidence that the art was spread from Europe southwards across Africa. There appear to have been three major areas of development in southern, eastern and northern Africa, and although there is some parallelism in the development, the differences seem to be greater than the similarities.

It is particularly remarkable that the most striking similarity both in style and subject should be between the art at the extremes of the geographical distribution – the eastern Spanish paintings and the southern African ones. That the other rock arts show little likeness to either of these traditions, although they lie between them, suggests that no connection exists, a conclusion which may be strengthened by the fact that some Australian rock paintings are comparable to both.

The fauna of southern Africa, unlike that of North Africa, has been unchanged since the middle of the Upper Pleistocene, so we cannot use the represented animals to establish a chronology for the paintings, with the exception, however, of the cattle and fat-tailed sheep, which cannot antedate the relatively recent arrival of the pastoral Hottentots and Bantu.

The earliest art consists of simple engravings, often scarcely visible. The earliest paintings too have weathered away, leaving only light animal-shaped silhouettes on the rock. The early paintings are characterized by their peacefulness; the art is naturalistic and there is no recognizably modern subject-matter. The later paintings are less carefully executed and include elaborate scenes of ceremonies, raids and battles. In the early phase of this period the different races seem to be co-existing peacefully, but the late phase, the paintings of which are mostly concentrated round the south-eastern part of South Africa, reflects a period of constant struggle. It is usually possible to distinguish Bushmen (short stature, painted in yellow, red or brown and carrying bows and arrows), Bantu (tall stature, usually painted in black with ornaments on the arms and legs and armed with spears and shields) and Europeans (recognizable by their characteristic clothing, and often shown with guns and horses). The Hottentots are represented as similar to the Bushmen, and are usually only distinguishable from them in scenes of fighting between the two groups, when they are shown as taller than the Bushmen, painted in red or brown and armed with bows and arrows or spears.

Many allegedly foreign influences have been claimed in the art. The Abbé Breuil in particular interpreted some subjects as Sumerians or Egyptians, yet none of these suggestions can be substantiated. *Ill. 34* Breuil's famous 'White Lady of the Brandberg' is certainly a male figure covered with white paint or eggshell beads[56] and paintings of figures wearing 'Sumerian cloaks' are in fact wearing fringed karosses like those of the mountain Bushmen and Basuto. Moreover, despite the large amount of excavation which has been carried out in southern Africa, no intrusive Mediterranean or Near Eastern artefacts have been found.

The great richness of these art forms in southern Africa has stimulated a great deal of study, and new sites are continually being discovered, though unfortunately there is no single agency responsible for recording them all. Different traditions prevail in different areas and numerous local style sequences have been described. In some areas it has been claimed that as many as seventeen styles could be placed in order of time by their regular occurrence in the same overlapping relationships, though more detailed and extensive studies have shown that these sequences are not consistent.[57] Indeed, Willcox has pointed out that in the Drakensberg, although monochrome paintings precede bichrome, and both precede polychrome, the monochrome style continues alongside the younger ones.[58]

Ill. 33 The peak of achievement in Bushman painting was undoubtedly in the polychrome paintings, which have a very restricted distribution in the south-east of South Africa. In this area two main periods are

60

32 Polychrome painting of a disguised Bushman hunting ostriches at Wittcberge, Herschel. Cape Province, South Africa W. 26 in. (After Stow and Bleek.)

distinguished, the pre- and post-Bantu, i.e. before and after the early seventeenth century. The polychrome paintings belong either just before or just after this divide; the very limited distribution suggests that the style was developed after the eastern Bushmen were restricted to this area by the incoming Bantu. These paintings show both deliberate composition of groups of figures and an understanding of foreshortening. Sometimes human figures are shown with animal heads. It has been suggested that these represent spirits, but the hunting of animals by means of such disguises is well documented among the Bushmen and elsewhere in Africa. One painting indeed shows a Bushman disguised as an ostrich but carrying his bow in his hand, while in other drawings hunters are shown with animal heads, presumably head-dresses. The success of such disguises, which permitted the hunter to get close to his prey, may have encouraged masked dancing for ritual purposes, but that is mere conjecture.[59]

Ill. 32

33 Shaded polychrome paintings of rooi rhebok at the Cavern, Site 1, Drakensberg, South-West Africa. The doe on the left turns her head to lick her thigh while the buck is apparently about to get up. Each painting is less than two inches long.

34 The so-called 'White Lady of the Brandberg', Tsisab Gorge, South-West Africa, is a dark-skinned male figure covered with white paint or ostrich egg-shell beads. Ht *c.* 15 in.

62

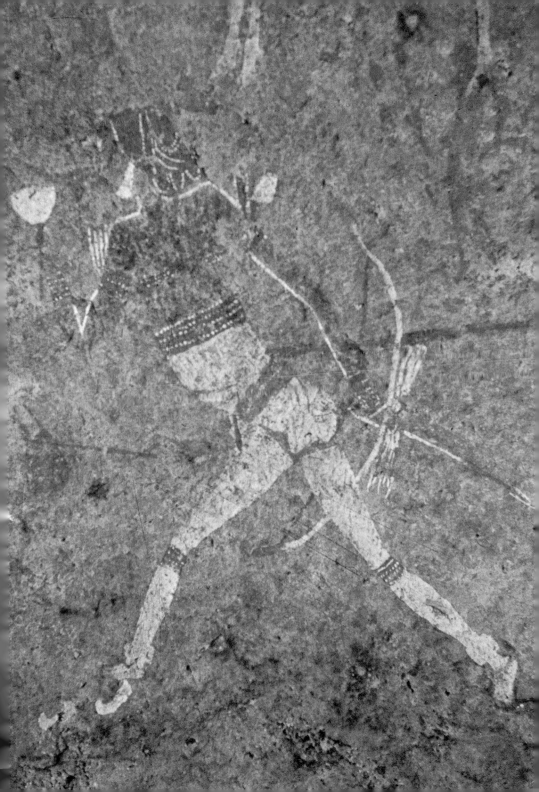

The rock art of eastern Africa is less well known than that of the other areas. The bulk of it seems to be fairly recent. Thousands of sites have been located in Tanzania, where a general sequence has been established, beginning with animals painted as monochrome silhouettes; followed by outlines which show an increasing attention to detail; then comes a phase of degeneration, the pose becoming stiffer and the outlines thick. Human figures appear mostly in the later phases, while geometric designs, similar to examples in Uganda, occur early in the sequence. Since all the Ugandan art (from only sixteen sites) seems not to be older than the beginning of the Christian era, it seems likely that the whole Tanzanian sequence is of similar age. From Zambia northwards, through Tanzania, Kenya, Uganda and Somalia, the latest phase is of white figures crudely daubed over the others. These are certainly quite recent; one example in Zambia even represents a motor car.[60]

One other example of rock art deserves to be mentioned, the cave of Mbafu in the Lower Congo. This is an area where Portuguese

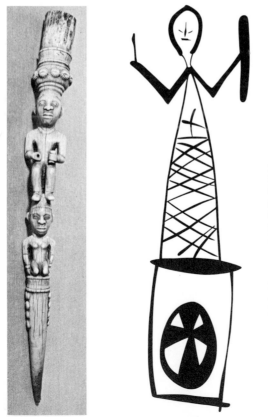

35 European influence on the Lower Congo is reflected in this elephant tusk carved by a BaKongo to represent a man in European dress, sitting above a kneeling woman. Manchester Museum (Forrester-Warden loan collection). L. $17\frac{1}{8}$ in.

36 Painting on a cave wall at Mbafu which probably represents Don Henrique, the first Congolese bishop who was consecrated in 1518. Ht 13 in.

influence was strong from the late fifteenth century and where the crucifix has become a power symbol used by chiefs when they sit in judgment. The crudely executed drawings on the cave walls show among other motifs a medal with a crucifix, a shield-shaped design with a cross and a XP motif, but of greatest interest is a group of figures, the central one of which wears a pectoral cross and stands on *Ill. 36* a platform bearing a Latin cross. These motifs seem likely to commemorate the consecration of Don Henrique, son of King Afonso I of the BaKongo, as the first Congolese bishop in 1518.[61]

Thus the rock art of Africa covers a period of perhaps seven thousand years, and shows us the changing life of the people up to the present day. There is much more for the archaeologist to do in placing this art on a firm chronological basis.

ANCIENT SCULPTURE

It is interesting to note that the general distribution of the rock art we have been discussing is, for the most part, outside the area of distribution of sculpture. It seems likely that these artists of the open savannas expressed themselves in paint and line, whereas the peoples of the West African forests and woodlands and of the Congo Basin preferred sculptural expression. While it is possible that the moister climate may have destroyed the evidence of painting, there are so very few engravings on rock that it seems probable that both forms of rock art were practically absent. Sculptures in stone are still lying around and, like the paintings, they are difficult to date directly.[62] Wood sculpture, however, does not survive long if not carefully and deliberately preserved, so in studying the history of African sculpture we are forced to rely on materials which endure neglect – chiefly terracotta and copper alloys (bronze and brass castings). Terracotta sculptures have been found in many parts of Africa, usually as isolated finds not apparently representing a continuous tradition, but in West Africa we have been fortunate in recovering evidence of two important sculptural traditions which allow us to observe the development of sculpture over a period of two and a half millennia.

The earliest sculptural tradition outside of Egypt is found in Nigeria. Terracotta sculptures, often on a large scale, of human and animal figures have been found, widely distributed across northern Nigeria. Such sculptures first came to light in tin-mines near the village of Nok in Zaria Province in the North Central State. Here

65

37 Terracotta head from a figure found during tin-mining at Nok, northern Nigeria. The eyes are represented in characteristic Nok style. The rings representing the hair, the pendant locks, and the hair-band are paralleled in the later sculptures from Ife. Jos Museum. Ht 8¼ in.

38 Dancer of the *gelede* society of Meko in western Yorubaland. The dances are intended to placate the witches in the community by entertaining them. The superstructures add to the entertainment value of the mask: this one represents a couple riding a motor cycle. It is part of the set carved for the 1969 series of *gelede* festivals. The eye of the mask resembles those on Nok sculptures; the pierced pupil is not intended for looking through, as can be seen, for the dancer's face is visible below the mask. The colourful costume makes effective use of imported plastic materials.

the sculptures were found in water-lain deposits, mixed up with finely polished stone axes and the remains of an iron-working industry. Radiocarbon dates from this deposit were A D 200 ± 50 (Y-474) from the layer in which the sculptures lay, and a series of dates, the latest of which was 925 ± 70 B C (Y-142-4), from the layer beneath the sculptures. More recently an occupation site of the culture has been found at Taruga, where there had been an extensive iron-working industry, for ten furnaces were found. Charcoal sealed in the base of one of them by iron slag gave a date of 300 ± 100 B C (I-3400) while the occupation layer in which Nok terracotta sculptures were found yielded dates of 440 ± 140 B C (I-2960) and 280 ± 120 B C (I-1459). Thus iron-working and terracotta sculpture were being carried out in the fourth or perhaps even the fifth century B,C.[63]

Terracotta is a plastic medium of sculpture, which calls for a different method of handling from wood. Wood is carved by removing pieces from the initial mass – a subtractive technique – whereas terracotta is usually built up a little at a time – an additive technique. The plastic medium of clay appears to be more responsive to delicacy of treatment, whereas wood carving tends towards cubistic representation. A few of the Nok sculptures show basic forms

Ill. 39   which would be more expected in wood: the mouth or beard forms a block projecting from the face, incised lines often mark the teeth and the edges of the lip. It appears that the Nok sculptures in terracotta are derived from a tradition of wood sculpture which is unknown to us since no carved wood of such antiquity has been preserved, nor can we guess how far back such a tradition might go, though it is natural to wonder whether some of the Tassili paintings, which are thought to represent masks and masked figures, might not

Ill. 29   reflect such an ancient tradition.

The Nok sculptures vary in size from about four inches up to four feet or more. It is difficult to establish the exact size of the larger pieces since they only survive incomplete. We have, for example, a head from Nok itself which is fourteen inches in height, implying a full length of four feet even if the head was exaggerated in scale; the lower part of a figure from Kuchamfa is almost two feet tall from the ground to the hips, again suggesting an overall height of not less than four feet. The limbs and bodies of the human figures are usually treated in a simplified way as tubes covered with strings of beads.

39 Fragment of the face of a tubular head in terracotta from Tonga Nok, northern Nigeria. Only the nose and mouth remain. The treatment of the mouth as a projecting block in which details are incised appears to reflect the existence of a wood-carving tradition in the area during the last four or five centuries B C. Jos Museum. Ht 6¼ in

The human head is usually cylindrical, spherical, or conical in form, with an elaborate head-dress and ears placed in a great variety of positions. The lips, ears, nostrils and the pupils of the eyes are usually pierced. The eye is represented as a segment of a sphere, with the upper lid usually horizontal, the lower lid forming a segment of a circle, which occasionally approximates to a triangle. The sweep of the curve of the lower lid is counterbalanced, often very precisely, in the curve of the eyebrow. The form of the eye is very similar to *Ill. 37* that on modern Yoruba *gelede* masks, where the piercing of the pupil is a stylistic feature, not a functional one, for the mask is worn on top of the head like a cap and the wearer looks out from between the clothing below the mask, as may be seen in *Ill. 38*. So far there is no evidence of this particular feature in the intervening period, so this may be an example of convergence.

The human figures from Nok are represented in a stylized manner whereas the animal figures are remarkably naturalistic, although both share the same kind of eye. Himmelheber was told by a modern Guro carver that he never carved a human face so that it resembled

69

40 Mask cast from almost pure copper in the naturalistic style for which Ife art is best known. This piece was clearly intended to be worn, perhaps in the burial rituals of a king of Ife. It is said always to have been kept on a shrine in the palace, and thus was for a long time the only example of Ife metal-casting known in the town. It is not surprising, therefore, that it was thought to represent Obalufon who is supposed to have introduced the technique to Ife. Ife Museum. Ht 13 in.

41 A group of highly stylized heads from various parts of Ife which appear to be contemporary with heads in an intensely naturalistic style. The second from the left shows a blend of a conical head shape and moderately naturalistic features. Ife Museum. Hts 5, $7\frac{1}{2}$, $6\frac{1}{2}$, $6\frac{3}{8}$ in.

42 Figure in brass of an Oni of Ife found at Ita Yemoo in 1958. Excavations at the site showed that contemporary terracotta sculptures in a similar style but larger in size had been abandoned by the twelfth century A D. Ife Museum. Ht $18\frac{3}{8}$ in.

any individual for fear of being accused of witchcraft; very possibly a similar idea accounts for the stylized treatment of human beings by the Nok sculptors, for they were clearly capable of naturalistic sculpture, as the animal figures show. This same contrast between more or less naturalistic animals and highly stylized human figures is found in the Franco-Cantabrian rock art of the Upper Old Stone Age, where too it probably reflects a similar fear of witchcraft accusations.

How long into the Christian era Nok sculpture persisted is very difficult to establish, but it seems to represent a seminal stage in the cultural history of West Africa for, although we cannot prove a connection, we find that the tubular head form set at an angle on a tubular neck occurs also among the undated stone sculptures at Esie,[64] among the sixteenth-century Afro-Portuguese ivories carved *Ill. 53* at Sherbro,[65] and among the *nomoli* figures of Sierra Leone (p. 98).[66] Again, the proportions of the body commonly found in African sculpture – large head and short legs – are seen in the small Nok figures which have survived in reasonably complete condition.

Several details of dress and of hair-style represented in the Nok sculptures are to be found to this day among the small groups of the Nigerian Plateau. A few groups now living in or close to the area of the Nok culture were making terracotta sculpture until very recently, for example the Tiv, the Dakakari and the Ham. Although the details of style are different, these may perhaps be the remains of a continuous tradition going back more than two millennia. However, no archaeological remains have yet been identified in the area which can fill the long gap in time between the flourishing of the Nok culture from the fourth century BC to perhaps the second or later AD and these nineteenth- and twentieth-century examples.

There is, however, a sculptural style which belongs chronologically in roughly the middle of this time gap, and which has many features in common with the Nok style. This is the art of the city of Ife, the religious, and earlier the political capital of the Yoruba peoples of South-western Nigeria. The art style of Ife is characterized by an idealized naturalism in both human and animal representations, yet alongside this there is, right through the whole period when Ife art *Ills. 40, 41* flourished, a tradition of extreme stylization. Occasionally the two strands are combined in, for example, a conical head with naturalistic features. Radiocarbon dates from the writer's excavations at Ita

Yemoo in Ife indicate that the terracotta sculptures found on one shrine were already broken by the twelfth century AD.[67] The two other groups of sculptures – one consisting of seven bronze castings, the other of seven terracotta figures – are to be considered contemporaneous on the evidence of archaeological stratigraphy. It should be noted, however, that this is the date when these pieces were deposited, not when they were made. How much older they may have been is not certain, but another site in Ife has provided five radiocarbon dates which range from the sixth to the tenth centuries, showing that Ife was occupied at a time which might well overlap that of the Nok culture, although we have no evidence yet that sculpture was being practised in Ife at this early date.[68] Moreover, Thurstan Shaw's excavations at Igbo-Ukwu in the East Central State of Nigeria have demonstrated that this rich collection of ornamental bronzes was deposited about the middle of the ninth century AD.[69] Although the art style and the composition of the metals are different from those of Ife, the fact that brilliantly skilful metalwork, both cast and forged, was being made about two hundred miles away supports the possibility of a similarly early date for the beginning of bronze-casting at Ife.

Ill. 42

Ills. 43, 44

A comparison of Nok and Ife sculptures, however, leaves one with little doubt that there is a cultural and an artistic connection between them, though the precise nature of the link remains obscure. These are the only two artistic traditions we know in the whole of Africa which have attempted human figure sculpture on a scale approaching life-size. The fragments of trunk and limbs are very similar indeed in their simplification, despite the great naturalism of Ife faces. In both styles the sculptures are sometimes set on a globular base; the hair is occasionally represented as rings, and similar pendant locks are represented. The figures are usually heavily beaded: not only are large numbers of anklets and bracelets worn, but the arrangement of beads on the chest is very similar in many cases in both traditions – a heavy rope of beads overlies many strings of smaller beads which cover the whole chest. This, of course, is a cultural rather than an artistic similarity, though the style of representation of the beads is often close in both. Both groups of artists show an interest in disease and deformity, a feature which is especially characteristic of Ibibio sculpture of the present day, which may also draw upon the Nok tradition as Bernard Fagg has suggested.[70] Between Nok and Ife

Ill. 37

43 Bronze altar stand excavated by Thurstan Shaw at Igbo-Ukwu, Nigeria. The castings from this site are very richly encrusted with decoration. This example has a male and female figure on opposite sides flanked with openwork panels featuring snakes and spiders. These castings were buried about the ninth century A D. Nigerian Museum, Lagos. Ht $11\frac{3}{4}$ in.

44 Many of the bronzes from Igbo-Ukwu were decorated with coloured beads of glass and stone. Below the flange snakes' heads appear through tubes, and face alternately upwards and downwards. This object is thought to have been the head of a ceremonial staff. Nigerian Museum, Lagos. Ht $6\frac{5}{8}$ in.

45 Terracotta head found by gold-miners in the Mokuro Stream, Ife. The bulging eyes, flat protrusive lips and stylized ears indicate its intermediate position between the naturalistic style of ancient Ife sculpture and that of Yoruba works of the present day. Ife Museum. Ht $7\frac{3}{4}$ in.

there appears to have been a shift of emphasis along the continuum of artistic expression between extreme stylization and extreme naturalism. Nok sculpture is predominantly stylized though the animals are naturalistically represented, while at Ife both human faces and animal figures are naturalistic, while the rest of the human figures are moderately stylized, and there are even some heads which are more highly stylized than those of Nok. Presumably this shift of the balance towards naturalism reflects a change in the philosophy of the Ife court and priesthood, throwing off the inhibitions on naturalistic representation of the human face.

Ill. 41

75

In the Ife art, however, it is possible to distinguish a large number of sculptures which show an increasing degree of stylization in the representation of the human face – the eyes begin to bulge, the lips to protrude as two horizontal projections while a variety of simplified forms is used to represent the ear. These three features, within a general tradition of moderate naturalism, are characteristic of modern Yoruba sculpture. In Ife sculpture it is possible to observe the rigorous naturalism of the Classical Period becoming more relaxed and increasingly stylized in the post-Classical works, so that we can

Ill. 45 observe a modern African sculptural style being born. Excavations in the Palace at Ilesha, twenty miles from Ife, revealed a nineteenth-

Ill. 46 century phase of this development of Yoruba sculpture. In this style the bulging eye reaches its limit as a hemisphere, a form which one still sees in some modern Yoruba sculptures.[71]

Archaeology then can bring us close to the present day, but for the last five centuries we can call upon other evidence as well. Sculptures of some antiquity may be found in modern use, as is certainly the case in Ife, though here it is usually a case of discontinuity of use – the antiquities have been found by accident and put to a new and often unrelated use. William Bascom and John Picton recently found an *egungun* mask in use in the Modakeke section of Ife which carried a

46 One of a large number of sculptures excavated by the author at Ilesha, twenty miles north-east of Ife. These sculptures, of lightly fired clay, appear to be of nineteenth-century date and are in a fully developed Yoruba style. Ife Museum. Ht 9½ in.

47 *Tellem* figure from the Dogon, encrusted with sacrificial matter. British Museum. Ht 19½ in.

48, 49 Nigeria is rich in traditions of casting copper alloys by the lost wax process, but their relationships and their antiquity are not always clear. This sculpture has given its name to the 'Huntsman style', one of William Fagg's group of 'Lower Niger Bronze Industries'. This piece was found in Benin, but is not in the Benin style. The omission of the lower part of the right leg is noteworthy. British Museum. Ht $14\frac{1}{2}$ in.

couple of small but fine terracotta heads among the animal skulls and other magical materials which adorned it. Among the Dogon, in the bend of the River Niger, large numbers of old wood carvings have long been known, which they call *tellem*. The Dogon believe that they were carved by an earlier and different group of people who occupied the same territory, but their style seems to be ancestral to that of the Dogon. A fragment of one was subjected to the radiocarbon test and found to date from 1470 ± 150 AD (Sa-61), roughly to the time of the earliest European explorations of the West African coast which afford us evidence of a different kind.[72]

Ill. 47

77

50 (*opposite*) Detail of the figure of a woman holding a fan (now bent) in her left hand. This is one of the largest bronze castings ever made in Africa, and is kept in the Nupe village on Jebba Island, to which it is said to have been brought from Idah by their great founder hero Tsoede in the early sixteenth century. Ht 45½ in.

51 (*above*) One of a group of cast bronze vessels in animal form collected among the Jukun by Arnold Rubin. These appear to be of ancient manufacture and had been dug up between Wukari and Bantaji about 1940. Nigerian Museum, Lagos. L. c. 6 in.

52 A number of bronze-casting traditions await investigation in Nigeria. This hippopotamus is one of a group of pieces thought to have been found in Enyong Division of the Southeastern State. Nigerian Museum, Lagos. L. 8½ in.

The European explorers on the coast were interested in the economic potential of Africa, and brought back slaves, gold, ivory and spices from their travels. They seem very rarely to have brought back works of art or even crafts. Probably the first art-work thus brought back was the group of objects in hybrid styles carved by African workmen after European models in the sixteenth century. There are about a hundred of these Afro-Portuguese ivories surviving, mostly in the form of elaborate salt-cellars, end-blown hunting-horns often deco-

Ill. 55   rated with European animals of the chase, spoons and forks. The spoons and forks are, apart from the decorative handles, essentially of sixteenth-century European form, and the arms of Portugal occur on the hunting-horns. Some of these ivories appear to have been carved by Benin sculptors[73] but most are in a style closely similar to

Ill. 53   that of the *nomoli* figures of Sierra Leone. Alan Ryder[74] has discovered in the Portuguese customs entries for 1504 to 1505 records of payments of duty on ivory spoons and salt-cellars brought back from the Guinea Coast. The ivories are always accompanied by rice and palm fibre bags or mats. According to Pacheco Pereira[75] (writing 1506–8), rice was bought by the Portuguese at this time only from Sherbro

53 *Nomoli* figure carved in soapstone and representing a man leaning against a backrest. These pieces resemble in style some of the Afro-Portuguese ivories (*Ill. 55*) and are thought to be of sixteenth-century date. Sierra Leone. Manchester Museum. Ht 11 in.

Island northwards to what is now Portuguese Guinea, and he mentions the Temne and the Bulom who live in this area as being skilled in making both ivory spoons and palm fibre mats. An Englishman, James Welsh, visited Benin in 1588, where he saw 'spoones of Elephants teeth very curiously wrought with divers proportions of foules and beasts made upon them'. Until the second decade of the seventeenth century, Ryder, reports, the Portuguese were still buying ivory spoons there.

Five of these spoons are still in the Wieckmann Collection in the Museum of the town of Ulm near Stuttgart, together with a raffia fibre bag. The catalogue of this collection was published in 1659. The source of the bag appears to have been recorded as Benin and it is interesting that raffia-weaving is mentioned with the ivory spoons in the Portuguese references to the Bulom, the Temne and the Bini. *Ill. 55*

This same collection also includes the earliest pieces of Yoruba sculpture to be brought to Europe: two ivory bracelets and a wooden tray which were collected at Ardra in modern Dahomey. The catalogue describes the bracelets as 'figured with divers toads and loathsome animals, such as the noblemen of the king of Ardra are accustomed to wear on their arms as a special ornament and mark of *Ills. 57–58* *Ill. 59*

54 *Bundu* masks made for the *Sande* Society which arranges the education of young Ménde girls in the responsibilities of adult life are probably the best-known wood sculptures from Sierra Leone. The mask is worn by a woman who, in this example, sees out through slits beside the jaw at the level of the mouth. Manchester Museum. Ht 15 in.

81

55 Handle of an ivory spoon in Afro-Portuguese style, representing two goats chewing leaves. Collected in the sixteenth century. Wieckmann Collection, Ulm Museum. Ht of section shown: $4\frac{3}{4}$ in.

distinction'. The tray is described as an 'offering board carved in relief with rare and loathsome devilish images, which the king of Ardra, who is a vassal of the king of Benin, together with the greatest officers and important men of the region, are accustomed to employ in fetish customs by making sacrifices on it to their gods. This offering board was furnished and used by the presently reigning King of Ardra himself.' The tone of these descriptions helps us to understand why so little was collected in the first four hundred years of contact with the African coast – such objects were viewed with horror as reflecting the depravity of the natives. No attempt at all was made to establish their real function. The tray was certainly not used in sacrifice, but for recording the signs indicated by the oracle in Ifa divination.[76]

What is noticeable about all three pieces is the close similarity of the artistic style from the first half of the seventeenth century up to the present day. The cow heads on one of the bracelets for example are closely similar to those carved on planks for ancestor altars in present-day Owo, while the human figures on the Ifa tray are rather like those on a door panel from Ijebu in the British Museum.[77]

Cf. Ill. 64

82

56 A modern board for Ifa divination from Dahomey. The colours and motifs should be compared with *Ill. 23*. The face at the top is said by Bascom to represent Eshu, the principle of uncertainty in the Yoruba pantheon. Linden Museum, Stuttgart. $9 \times 7\frac{1}{2}$ in.

57, 58 Two ivory bracelets collected at Ardra during the first half of the seventeenth century. One represents snails and frogs; the other . has birds and cow heads alternating. Yoruba. Wieckmann Collection, Ulm Museum. Max. diams: $3\frac{1}{8}$ and $3\frac{7}{8}$ in.

59 Tray used in Ifa divination collected at Ardra (Allada) in Dahomey during the first half of the seventeenth century. Yoruba. Wieckmann Collection, Ulm Museum. $22 \times 13\frac{3}{4}$ in.

There are four stone figures in the Luigi Pigorini Museum in Rome which are reputed to have been brought back to Rome from *Ill. 60* the Lower Congo about 1695. These too are very similar to their recent counterparts, the *mintadi*, carvings in soft stone made by the BaKongo to act as guardians over graves.[78] Some of the very recent stone carvings show Western influences: they represent soldiers, drummers, Europeans and once even a sewing-machine, but the earlier pieces from the eighteenth and nineteenth centuries are all fairly similar to each other. This, of course, is the area where the *Ill. 36* Mbafu paintings are, and where contact with Europeans has a long if discontinuous history. It is reassuring to find that these contacts were not entirely destructive.

Very few pieces seem to have been collected during the eighteenth and early nineteenth centuries, when the slave trade was at its height. However, when attempts were made to administer various parts of Africa, a number of works were gathered and sent to Europe, often as

84

61 Staff of office and two figures, BaJokwe. The figure on top of the staff wears the hair-dressing of a chief, simpler renderings of which are seen on the other pieces. British Museum. Hts $11\frac{3}{4}$, $13\frac{1}{4}$, 11 in.

60 Soapstone figure collected on the Lower Congo about 1695. Soapstone is very soft and easily damaged by blows but not prone to decay by weathering so that old carvings in this medium look quite new. Similar sculptures (called *mintadi*) are made in the area today by the BaKongo, to guard the graves of their ancestors. Luigi Pigorini Museum, Rome.

62 This BaJokwe chair shows constructional features copied from sixteenth-century Portuguese prototypes. The genre scenes however are in characteristic BaJokwe style as is the face on the backrest which represents the male mask Chihongo, symbol of wealth. Decoration with imported upholstery nails is also found on chiefs' chairs made in Ghana, which also evolved from European prototypes. British Museum. Ht 20 in.

63 Ivory bracelet used in Ife. The flange is pierced for attaching ornaments which have been lost. Ife Museum. $3\frac{1}{4} \times 2\frac{5}{8}$ in. Ht $1\frac{3}{4}$ in.

64 Ivory bracelet carved in the Yoruba town of Owo but collected in Benin. The elephant head in the centre is very similar to the cow head on the Ulm bracelet (*Ill. 58*). Museum für Völkerkunde, Berlin. Ht $6\frac{15}{16}$ in.

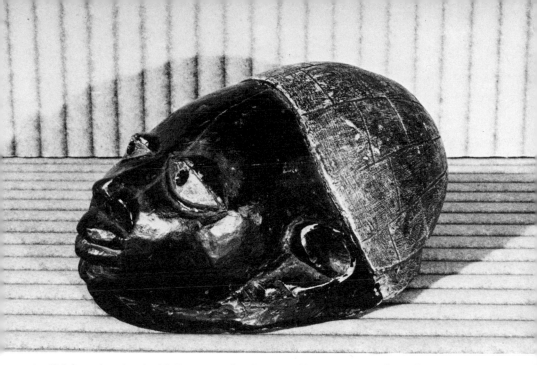

65 *Gelede* mask, painted with European oil-paints, seized between 1864 and 1870 by Governor Glover from a small Yoruba town which he destroyed. Manchester Museum. L. 13 in.

examples of heathenish practices, to encourage support for missionary societies. An example is the *gelede* mask shown in *Ill. 65* now in the Manchester Museum, but formerly belonging to the Church Missionary Society, to which it was given by Governor John H. Glover who took it, according to the label, 'from a heathen temple in a small town which was destroyed' by him. Glover was Lieutenant-Governor in 1864 and Administrator from 1866 to 1870, so it was presumably taken about this period. It is interesting to note that at this early date it appears to have been coloured with imported oil-paint.

A fine headpiece from the Cross River area now in the Nigerian *Ill. 66* Museum at Lagos, earlier in the Bankfield Museum at Halifax and before that in the Whitby Museum, may have been acquired in pleasanter circumstances, since it was collected by Consul John Beecroft in 1861. Even as early as 1820 a Yoruba staff for Shongo, the thunder god, had reached Switzerland, while in 1854 the British Museum had acquired a very new-looking pair of Yoruba twin figures, *ibeji*, probably from Abeokuta.[79] Perhaps rather later, a

87

66 Skin-covered headpiece, with metal teeth, collected by Governor Beecroft in 1861 at Old Calabar. Nigerian Museum, Lagos. Ht 10½ in.

Ill. 68

Ill. 67

very fine single figure of the same kind, came into the hands of a German collector, Georg Emil Schüz, who owned it for some time before his death in 1877. Robert Thompson has told me that it was carved in Ilaro, possibly by a linear predecessor of Onipasanobe. Towards the end of the century members of the family of the Ijo King Ockiya of the old trading port of Brass in the Niger Delta were converted to Christianity and gave a group of large carvings representing deceased members of the family to the missionaries, who sent them to their London headquarters, from where they were later dispersed. Their striking style is regarded by William Fagg as having been inspired by the figureheads of European sailing-ships, which must have been a common sight in Brass for centuries.[80] Once again, European influence, as in the Afro-Portuguese ivories, appears to have been felicitous.

The pieces we have been discussing were few in number and were regarded primarily as curios. The first African art to make a substantial impact in Europe was the vast quantity of bronze castings and ivory carvings which were seized by the Royal Navy as reparations in the course of the Benin Punitive Expedition of 1897.[81] It was immediately recognized that there was considerable skill and artistry in Africa, and a number of still-valuable books were written on them, notably H. Ling Roth's general study *Great Benin*, published in Halifax in 1903, and the catalogues *Antiquities from the City of Benin . . . in the British Museum* (London, 1899), by C. H. Read and O. M. Dalton, and *Antique Works of Art from Benin* (London, 1900), by A. H. Lane-Fox Pitt-Rivers, describing his own collection. It was not long after

67 Two large wooden figures from the old trading port of Brass in the Niger Delta, representing members of the family of the Ijo 'King' Ockiya. They appear to be based on ships' figureheads, and it is probably significant that the arms are carved separately and attached. Left: Manchester Museum. Ht 33$\frac{1}{2}$ in. Right: University Museum, Philadelphia, Pennsylvania. Ht *c.* 36 in.

68 Twin figure probably from Ilaro in Yorubaland which was in the collection of Georg Emil Schüz of Stuttgart before 1877. John Picton informs me that as the birth of twins is regarded as an unusual event, the diviner is consulted by the parents. He may advise the making of a pair of such figures, or this may be postponed till one twin dies. The figure of the dead twin is ritually fed at the same time as the survivor. There is thus no standard practice prescribed. Linden Museum, Stuttgart. Ht 10 in.

69 Large skin-covered Janus head from the Cross River area. This type of mask seems to have originated among the Ekoi but is now used by a number of neighbouring peoples. There are many fine examples in museum collections which lack collector's data. This one was presented by the Davyhulme County School to the Manchester Museum, but no earlier history is known. Ht 25 in.

this that Leo Frobenius set out on his 'Inner Africa Expeditions', and the deliberate collecting in Africa for the enrichment of European collections had begun. If these pieces had not been collected many of them would certainly have been destroyed by now, but it is most regrettable that records were rarely kept of the precise source of any objects, a practice which dealers in such pieces have continued 'in order to protect their sources of supply'. Even Frobenius records in different books the same piece as coming from completely different places.[82] This lack of documentation of museum collections, both public and private, inevitably limits any study based on them, as Kjersmeier pointed out in explanation of his inability to give more than a general idea of the sculpture of the Ibo, Ibibio, Ijo and Efik.[83] All the major ethnographic collections in the world suffer from this inadequate documentation of important pieces. In order to remedy it, research workers commonly study museum collections in conjunction with their field-work, so that each may throw light on the other.

Although very little art was brought back from Africa until the end of the last century, we can glean some information from the literature of African exploration. One of the first travellers to write

70 Three doors from the Awka area, to the east of the River Niger, where the Ibo carvers have shown a special talent for geometric ornament. British Museum. Hts $43\frac{1}{2}$, $40\frac{1}{2}$ and 33 in.

71 Pottery sculpture for the altar of Ifijioku, the giver and protector of yams, from the Riverain Ibo village of Osisa west of the River Niger. This is one of several examples taken to England about 1880. The man's wives hold their children while other figures beat a gong, carry a box of offerings and sacrifice an animal. The lids of the offering box and of the rectangular chest in front of the group are both removable. Nigerian Museum, Lagos. Ht 19 in.

about Africa was Ibn Battuta, who has left us a record of masked dancers whom he saw during his visit to the Mali Empire, in Mali, now believed to be the town of Nyani, in modern Bambaraland. He describes the incident in the following words: 'On feast days . . . the poets[84] come in. Each of them is inside a figure resembling a thrush, made of feathers, and provided with a wooden head with a red beak, to look like a thrush's head. They stand in front of the Sultan in this ridiculous make-up and recite their poems.' Their poems exhort the King to recall the good deeds of his predecessors, and imitate them so that the memory of his good deeds will outlive him. 'I was told that this practice is a very old custom amongst them, prior to the introduction of Islam, and that they have kept it up.'[85]

72 Mask from the Afikpo Ibo, used in plays of social comment during the dry season. These masks, called *mba*, represent girls and are worn in pairs by men in a performance in which one represents a girl whose behaviour is being mimicked by the other, a boy dressed as a girl. Manchester Museum. Ht 20 in.

73 *Agbogho Mmwo*, a Maiden Spirit mask worn with an elaborate appliqué costume by the middle grade of the men's society at funerals and festivals in which the masquerader mimics women's activities. Nigerian Museum, Lagos. Ht 20$\frac{1}{4}$ in.

The early European travellers tell us very little about the sculpture which the Africans made for their own use. Pacheco Pereira, for example, repeatedly refers to the Africans as 'idolaters' but does not describe their 'idols'. His descriptions of the local way of life are very brief and refer chiefly to the economy. Describing the western corner of the Niger Delta about 1506–8 he says: 'there is nothing on which to make a profit', and goes on: 'the Negroes of this country are idolaters and are circumcised without knowing why, and have no laws; and because these are things which do not have much to do with the subject one can be excused from writing about them'.[86] In the next paragraph he writes of Benin: 'There are many abuses in this people's way of life, their fetishes and idolatries which I leave undescribed so as not to be prolix.'[87] Nevertheless, he does tell us that the people of Benin have marks over their eyebrows which distinguish them from other peoples in the area.[88] The Bini do not wear such marks nowadays though they are commonly represented in Benin sculpture. He also tells us an interesting story about the Isles of Los, opposite

76 *Ikenga* collected early this century among the Igala. Its form appears to be derived from a northern Ibo prototype like the one on the left of the preceding illustration. City Museum, Ipswich. Ht *c.* 18 in.

74, 75 Two Ibo *ikenga*, or personal shrines at which the owner ensures the continuing power of his right hand, i.e. of his physical as opposed to his mental powers. The cult is found on both sides of the Lower Niger. The scarification over the forehead is the *itchi* mark of rank among the Ibo. British Museum. Hts 11¼, 9½ in.

77, 78, 79 The masks of the Igala show a great variety of forms. The masks shown are called *Amda* (*above left*), *Ogbodo* (*left*) and *Ikpelikpa* (*above*). Nigerian Museum, Lagos. Hts 14, 21 and 24 in.

Conakry. Their modern name is evidently derived from the name Pacheco Pereira uses: 'Ilhas dos Idolos.' 'This name was given to them because when the islands were discovered, a great many idols were found which the inhabitants were in the habit of taking and worshipping when they went to sow their rice.'[89] This account is not very precise, but it seems to echo the findings of sculptures of *Ill. 53* soft stone in the lands of the Mende (who call them *nomoli*) and the Kissi (who call them *pomdo*), who set them up in the rice-fields to protect the crop and make it prosper. Indeed, it is reported that the *nomoli* are expected to steal rice plants from the neighbouring fields to this end, and that they are beaten if they do not do this successfully.

The first illustration of anything resembling an African mask is in François Froger's *Relation d'un Voyage fait en 1695, 1696 et 1697 au Côtes d'Afrique* (Paris, 1698) where he represents 'the costume of the circumcised' round the River Gambia: a figure who appears to be wearing an antelope mask which looks rather like one type used by the *Ills. 80, 81* Guro. Froger tells us that the King 'wore on his head a wickerwork cap decorated with several rows of coral beads and a pair of cowhorns', and that 'the circumcised are permitted to wear a similar cap for a

80 'The costume of the circumcised' around the River Gambia in the late seventeenth century as represented by Froger. This is probably the earliest illustration of an African mask in the European literature about Africa.

81 Mask representing an antelope used in the *Zamle* Society dances of the Guro of Ivory Coast. Froger's illustration appears to represent a mask of similar form, though it cannot be identical in view of the distance (almost fifteen hundred miles) which separates them. Moreover the *zamle* mask is worn vertically in front of the face. British Museum. Ht 18¾ in.

week after their circumcision, which permits them to perpetrate all the crimes imaginable without anyone daring to complain about it'.

At all periods the writers describe the kinds of houses they observe, and eventually they provide drawings of them. *Les Voyages du Sieur Lemaire aux Isles Canaries, Cap-Verd, Sénégal et Gambie* (Paris, 1695) shows a drawing of houses based on Lemaire's sketches. One of the houses is sectioned to show the bed, and the text gives a very detailed description. In 1714 Godefroy Loyer in his *Relation du voyage du Royaume d'Issiny, Côte d'Or, Païs de Guinée en Afrique* describes three different types of houses, one of them round, another square and of one or two storeys, while the third is described as a 'miserable hut made of reeds and palm leaves, so low that a man can scarcely stand up inside' yet the illustrations are hardly distinguishable from each other, or from Lemaire's, yet Hirschberg says they were 'obviously prepared from the author's sketches'.[90] In contrast in 1719 Peter Kolb in *Caput Bonae Spei Hodiernum* (Nürnberg) describes the building of Hottentot houses with what are almost engineering drawings.

The most interesting series of travellers' illustrations and descriptions, however, refer to Benin. Many of the drawings, of course,

99

82 The burial of the King of Benin according to Pieter de Marees at the turn of the sixteenth and seventeenth centuries. There is a faint possibility that what the artist has represented as real heads were in fact bronze castings.

83 View of the city of Benin published by Dapper in 1668. Sculptures made by the Bini themselves confirm the accuracy of many of the details.

were not made on the spot but prepared from the descriptions and so have little documentary value. Sometimes there is reason to suspect that the observer may have misinterpreted what he saw. For example, the illustration of the burial of the King which accompanies Pieter de Marees's account of Benin published in 1603 in DeBry's *India Orientalis* shows human heads placed on top of sticks round the grave, *Ill. 82* the text informing us that these are the heads of a wife, a child and servants who are willing to accompany him to the next world. Now von Luschan[91] publishes a photograph taken in Benin at the time of the Punitive Expedition which shows sculptured heads of an early style placed on the brackets of a tall staff, and he suggests that this was what de Marees was mistakenly describing. However, later Benin heads are furnished with a flange and are massively made so that they can stand directly on the altar and support carved ivory tusks which lean against the wall behind. Moreover, I have seen a human skull on several occasions lying on an altar in Benin City, and von Luschan shows a whole row of them on another altar in 1897. So there are some grounds for wondering whether the bronze heads may not have been used later in place of real heads. If von Luschan's interpretation is right (though we cannot be sure that the bronze heads were not placed on the staff by a member of the Punitive Expedition), this is the earliest illustration we have of Benin art.

Less controversial is the famous view of Benin City published by Olfert Dapper in *Nauwkeurige Beschrijvinge der Afrikaansche Gewesten* *Ill. 83*

84 Bronze casting from Benin representing a dwarf like those shown in Dapper's illustration. William Fagg suggests that they are probably from the early period of Benin bronze-casting, before 1600. Museum für Völkerkunde, Vienna. Ht 23$\frac{1}{4}$ in.

Ill. 84

Ills. 85, 86
Ill. 87

(Amsterdam) in 1668. This shows the King in procession with musicians and warriors. The accuracy of the drawing has been confirmed in a number of ways; for example, dwarfs shown with the King are also represented in two of the finest figure sculptures we have from Benin, but it is the architecture of the Palace which is of greatest interest. Ling Roth commented 'This is another fancy picture'[92], but not only are the tall pyramidal towers also represented on the bronze plaques, but the cast-bronze leg of a large bird, which can only be from one of those shown standing on the apex of the tower has been found in the Palace. It is Dapper too who first refers to the bronze plaques. He speaks of 'wooden pillars, from top to bottom covered with cast copper, on which are engraved the pictures of their war exploits and battles, and are kept very clean'.[93] A few years later, in 1701, David Nyendael visited Benin. He describes the Palace more fully than Dapper, referring to the 'wooden turret like a chimney about sixty or seventy feet high. At the top of all is fixed a large copper snake whose head hangs downwards. This serpent is very well cast or carved, and is the finest I have seen in Benin.' These serpents are represented on the plaques, and sixteen or seventeen heads of them survive, one of which was excavated by John Goodwin inside the area of the former Palace.[94] Nyendael describes passing through a big courtyard to a gallery beyond, 'half thrown down by a thunderstorm since which it has not been rebuilt'. Beyond was another gallery in which the roof was supported on human figures 'but so wretchedly carved that it is hardly possible to distinguish whether they are most like men or beasts; notwithstanding which my guides were able to distinguish them into merchants, soldiers, wild beast hunters, etc. Behind a white carpet we are also shewn eleven men's heads cast in copper, by much as good an artist as the former carver, and upon every one of these there is an elephant's tooth, these being some of the King's gods.'[95] He later refers to seven more tusks on ivory pedestals. This is the most detailed account of the Palace so far given by the European travellers. It includes the first description of the heads and the tusks upon them, and the first account of the serpents on the turrets. Why does he not refer to the birds on top of the turrets, or to the plaques? It may be that the plaques were formerly in the gallery which had been ruined by the thunderstorm. Many of them are bent and many are incomplete, perhaps as a result of the collapse of the building. It is generally thought that they had been removed to safer

85 Bronze box representing a section of the palace with a tower, python and ibis. Two armed Portuguese and another ibis (formerly two) stand on the ridge of the roof. Museum für Völkerkunde, Berlin. L. 24 in.

87 Cast-bronze leg from the figure of an ibis which formerly stood on top of a tower of the palace. Found on an altar in the Palace in Benin. L. c. 24 in.

86 Bronze plaque cast in Benin representing a gateway of the royal palace surmounted by a turret which carries a python. Many heads and some body segments of these pythons survive. One of R. E. Bradbury's informants told him that at the time of the Benin Expedition, the body fragments were used by the young court attendants to stand upon while they bathed. The columns supporting the shingled roof carry bronze plaques representing Portuguese faces, while the feet of a bird can be seen at the top of the tower. Museum für Völkerkunde, Berlin. Ht 19 in.

88 Bronze head of the late period of Benin art; a massive casting intended to support an ivory tusk on an ancestor altar in the Palace. The projecting decorations on the crown are said in Benin to have been introduced by the Oba Osemwede (1816–48). The head cannot therefore be earlier than this time. British Museum. Ht 20⅛ in.

89 The reigning King of Benin, Oba Akenzua II, photographed during the *Emobo* ceremony in 1959. He wears a crown and collar of coral beads similar to those represented in the bronze head in *Ill. 88*. His shirt is also of coral beads. He strikes an ivory gong and wears an ivory armlet and has low-relief plaques of ivory round his waist.

90 (*left*) This mask is one of seven which were used in the cult of the water spirit Igbile at Ughoton (Gwatto), the old port of Benin. They were brought out to invoke the help of Igbile against the Punitive Expedition in 1897. Their style appears to be derived from that of the Western Ijo of the Niger Delta, via the Ilaje Yoruba, for the songs used in the cult are in the Ilaje dialect. British Museum. Ht 31$\frac{1}{8}$ in.

91 (*right*) The art style of the Benin court was derived, together with the technique of bronze-casting, from Ife. Gradually, however, it has influenced the popular style of Benin wood sculpture, as is apparent in this *ekpo* mask where the face is framed by a rectangle of beads obviously copied from the royal ancestor heads. Ife Museum. Ht 11 in.

storage before Nyendael arrived, for they were kept like a card index up to the time of the Punitive Expedition, and referred to when there was a dispute about courtly etiquette, as we know from an old chief who was a Palace attendant before the expedition. The storm had probably blown down the birds from the tops of the turrets too. Yet, as William Fagg has pointed out to me, it is quite possible that the supports of the roof in the second gallery were not wood carvings but the plaques themselves, many of which do indeed show merchants, soldiers and hunters. It is interesting to observe that although Nyendael remarks on the excellence of workmanship, he shows little appreciation of Bini art.

In Benin, of course, we have more to draw on than the travellers' accounts and so are able to gauge their accuracy. Clapperton writing

92 The kings of the BaMbala or Bushongo, the best known of the BaKuba chiefdoms, were commemorated in wooden figures, each bearing a symbol to indicate which individual was represented. This is Shamba Balongongo, the ninety-third Nyimi who reigned about 1600–20, though it seems unlikely that the carving is contemporary with him. In front of him is a board for the game of *wari*, nowadays widespread in Africa, which he is said to have introduced to wean his people away from excessive gambling. British Museum. Ht $21\frac{1}{2}$ in.

93 The NDengese who live across the Sankuru River to the north of the BaKuba have taken over and reinterpreted their royal ancestor figures, elongating the whole form of the sculpture and ornamenting the arms and trunk with scarification patterns. Musée Royal de l'Afrique Centrale, Tervuren. Ht $54\frac{3}{4}$ in.

94 Wooden figure from the Shongo shrine of the King of Oyo at Koso. Its name is *ere Alafin Shongo*, carving of or for King Shongo, who was one of the first kings of Oyo and who has since become identified with thunder and lightning. According to Philip Allison, who collected this piece, such a figure used to be made for each new king who visited the shrine at Koso at an early stage in his installation ceremonies, where he was crowned with a cloth crown which was left behind on one of the figures in the shrine. The king is never allowed to visit the shrine again. This figure is said to have been brought in 1837 from Koso at Old Oyo to the new site of Koso. Nigerian Museum, Lagos. Ht 38 in.

95 Wooden housepost representing a woman in an unusually curvilinear stance, bought by the author in Oyo whither it was claimed to have been brought by refugees from Old Oyo which collapsed in 1837. Ife Museum. Ht of figure: $40\frac{1}{2}$ in. Ht of post: 78 in.

of Old Oyo in 1826 says 'the people . . . are fond of ornamenting their doors, and the posts which support their verandahs, with carvings; and they have also statues or figures of men and women, standing in their courtyards. The figures carved on the posts and doors are various; but principally of the boa snake, with a hog or antelope in his mouth; frequently men taking slaves, and sometimes a man on horseback leading slaves.'[96] These motifs still occur in Ills. 226–29 Yoruba sculpture but the only houseposts I was able to find at Old Oyo were carved into baluster-like forms, with no representation. A number of sculptures in new Oyo, however, were said to have been brought from Old Oyo.[97]   Ills. 94, 95

We do have one example where we not only have a description and a picture of a work of art, but we can identify the object itself

today. This is the fine bronze mask still worn by the Ata of Idah on
ceremonial occasions. It is a late fifteenth- or early sixteenth-century
casting from Benin, which Commander William Allen described
during Lander's last expedition of 1832–33 in this way: 'In his lap.
and suspended from his neck, was a gilt representation – or libel – of
the human face, very like the "man in the moon".'[98] The libel is
rather perpetrated by Allen on a fine work of art, as we can see by
comparing his drawing with the original.

Ills. 96, 97

The purely historical, written, sources are thus of limited value in
themselves, but where they can be used in conjunction with other
data, they may prove valuable. Dapper's and Nyendael's accounts
of Benin allow us to infer that the casting of the plaques ceased about
the end of the seventeenth century, and this fact is one of the points
to which William Fagg has been able to anchor his chronology of
Benin art.[99]

In general it is evident from this survey that we must look primarily
to archaeology to reveal information about the history of African art,
but we are likely to get the most valuable insights in the later centuries
when archaeology, history (oral as well as written) and museum
collections can be used conjointly.

96 Commander William Allen's drawing of the Ata of Igala in 1832–33. He is wearing a mask round his neck which Allen described as 'a gilt representation – or libel – of the human face, very like the "man in the moon"'.

97 The Ata of Igala still wears the mask which Allen saw. It is called *Ejube auilo*, the eye which brings fear to other eyes, and is kept brightly polished. It is a Benin work of the late fifteenth or early sixteenth century, a period when there were substantial contacts between the two kingdoms. There are slits below the eyes which indicate that it was intended for wear over the face, a feature found on similar Benin masks in ivory, but not in bronze. In this feature it may be compared with the Ife mask in *Ill. 40*. Property of the Ata of Igala, Idah. Ht 11½ in.

EGYPT IN AFRICA

In the history of African art, as in the history of African culture as a whole, the effects of Islam and Christianity are very clear, but some writers have seen older influences which are more difficult to prove, notably those from Egypt, which although geographically a part of Africa is more usually regarded as falling within the cultural orbit of the Middle East. The scientific study of the Egyptian past has itself a long and distinguished history. A great deal was already known about ancient Egypt at the beginning of the present century, when scientific investigation of the peoples and cultures of Africa was still in its infancy. There was no chronological framework for African history and the sources of African culture were unknown. It is hardly surprising therefore that, when evidence came to light of considerable cultural achievements among African peoples, they were commonly attributed to influence from ancient Egypt despite the great gap in time. Moreover, the extreme Diffusionist school of W. J. Perry and Elliot Smith, which sought to derive all the higher civilizations of the world from ancient Egypt, was very influential.[100] Unfortunately, traces of this influence still persist in many writers. Margaret Trowell refs often to parallels between African sculpture and ancient Egyptian, suggesting that this is evidence of Egyptian influence in the rest of Africa.[101] The variety of divine Kings found in West and East Africa have all been thought to derive from ancient Egypt.[102]

Nowadays we know more about Africa, and can see more clearly the relationship between Egypt and the rest of the continent. Paul Bohannan expresses it this way: 'What happened in Egypt is that a strong Asian influence was stamped upon a basically African culture, giving rise to Egyptian civilization. A warning must be issued: "African culture" has nothing to do with forms of social organization, economy, polity, religion and the like. As we learn more and more about the cultures and civilizations of Africa, we realize that by these criteria Egypt lay culturally as well as geographically between Africa and Asia. Egyptian religion can be best understood only by reference to African religion; many other aspects of Egyptian history and polity are illuminated by African ethnography. It has been stylish in the past to assume that all these social and cultural forms were invented in Egypt and spread to other parts of Africa. Today we know that such was an oversimplification: Egypt was basically an African culture, with intrusions of Asian culture.'[103] The resulting culture flourished with the characteristic vigour of a hybrid.

The art of pre-Dynastic Egypt shows essentially African characteristics. The bowl shown in *Ill. 98*, dating from about 3100 BC, bears a painting of a boat in a simplified, highly stylized form which is in harmony with the much later paintings in caves round Lake Victoria, while the engraved bull shown in *Ill. 100* would be at home among the rock engravings of the Sahara.

Ill. 99

The statuary of later periods has all the characteristics of developed Egyptian style, yet it retains from pre-Dynastic times onwards a rigidity of form, a frontality[104] of pose, a lack of facial expression, and an absence of any clear indication of the age of the subject: features which are characteristic of most African figure sculpture.

In function too, these Egyptian statues are very similar to ancestor figures from many parts of Africa: they act as a repository of supernatural force, in particular they provide a residence for all eternity for the spiritual essence of the man represented.[105] 'Art for the Egyptian is a completely practical affair, designed not to move the emotions of the spectator for whom in any case it was not produced: but to ensure by magic means the immortality of the person repre-

98 Late Predynastic Egyptian pot with a boat and concentric arcs painted in red. From Nag' el Deir. Lowie Museum of Anthropology, University of California, Berkeley. Ht 9 in.

99 Part of a rock painting at Nyero, Teso district, Uganda showing parts of two canoes and concentric circles in red. The more complete canoe is 30 in. long. (After Posnansky.)

100 Late Predynastic Egyptian pot with a drawing of a bull incised upon it. From El Ahaiwah. Lowie Museum of Anthropology, University of California, Berkeley. Ht 10 in.

sented. The naturalistic form which Egyptian art often took, and the high degree of technical skill with which it was fashioned should not blind us to the fact that the ideas underlying it are nearer to . . . Africa than they are to Periclean Athens or to Renaissance Italy. . . . Each tomb statue was completed by undergoing a magical ritual which ensured that it became imbued with the spirit of the dead man . . . this consecration was effected upon a sculptural form which was an ideal representation of the sitter. . . . At whatever age the Egyptian may have died, he is shown in the full prime of a successful life . . . the realistic rendering of the muscles of the torso and limbs, and the apparent attempt at careful portraiture cannot disguise the fact that the conception is 'primitive', and that we are confronted with a perceptual, rather than a visual representation of the human form.'[106] These characteristics put Egyptian sculpture firmly within the African orbit. Far from being a potent source of influence in African art, Egyptian art is seen to be a local manifestation of a widespread African tradition.

This does not mean, however, that no artistic or other ideas have spread from Egypt to the rest of Africa,[107] but rather that we should show a reasonable caution in identifying them. In particular, as art historians, we need to pay very careful attention to chronology. To infer direct connections, without the evidence of intervening links, between Egyptian (or Roman or Phoenician) objects and others

101 Two *akua mma*, dolls from Ashanti which express the Ashanti ideal of beauty: a long neck and a round flat face with a high forehead and a small mouth. They are carried by expectant mothers who should not look upon any deformity (even a badly carved figure) for fear their child should resemble it. Conversely, by gazing up these expressions of idealized beauty the child is encouraged to be beautiful too. British Museum. Ht 13, 12½ in.

102 Terracotta heads excavated by Dr Oliver Davies at Ahinsan, southern Ashanti. These sculptures date from the late sixteenth and seventeenth centuries and appear to be ancestral in their artistic conventions to the more recent *akua mma* sculptures. University of Ghana. Hts 5 to $5\frac{7}{8}$ in.

made two or three or four millennia later in Africa is dangerous. It has been claimed for example that the *akua ba* doll of Ashanti is derived from the *ankh*, the Egyptian symbol of life.[108] None of the existing dolls is likely to be older than the nineteenth century; the immediate ancestors of their form appear to be the terracotta sculptures

Ill. 101

Ill. 102 found on a number of sites in Ashanti such as Ahinsan where they date from the late sixteenth and seventeenth centuries, yet these seem to have little in common with the *ankh* symbol. Too little regard is paid to the possibility of convergence, of the development of similar forms from dissimilar origins. Single traits may occur in several unrelated cultures. If form, meaning and function are similar in societies in which contact is known to have occurred at the relevant period, then we may legitimately infer an influence, though the direction of the influence may not always be clear. Without chronological controls the claim that African institutions are copied from Egyptian ones can certainly not be supported, especially as the prototypes are usually collected at random from the entire history of Egypt. When Africa was under colonial domination, it was understandable that many of its sons should have attempted to show that their own cultures drew on the same sources as the cultures of the European powers;[109] it is less understandable that European and American writers should still continue to follow the same line, unless they cannot believe that anything good ever came out of black Africa. With independence, a new generation of African scholars has grown up, who take justifiable pride in discovering the history of their own people with objective scholarship; fortunately, these include art historians.

103 Fanti doll, clearly related in form to the Ashanti *akua ba*. It has been claimed that both types of doll are Ashanti, and that the round-headed type is worn when a girl is desired and the rectangular-headed type when a boy is wanted, but in fact they are the work of different peoples. Linden Museum, Stuttgart. Ht $13\frac{5}{16}$ in.

CHAPTER FOUR

African Architecture

Architecture is a field in which remarkable achievements have been made in Africa, yet until recently it was the subject of no more than passing comment or of desultory study at most. We still do not have a single comprehensive study of the whole field of African architecture, though we do have a very complete study of the homes of the Fali of northern Cameroun[110] and an interesting account of traditional Ashanti architecture.[111] Several major studies of specific areas are currently under way and we can look forward to their eventual publication. However, Herta Haselberger has discussed West African architecture in general, while Julius Glück has provided an outline of African architecture as a whole.[112]

It is difficult to decide where mere building ends and architecture begins. The windbreaks used as a shelter by the Bushmen are perhaps hardly even to be considered building; the simple round beehive hut of flexible branches covered with leaves such as the Pygmies build can scarcely be considered architecture. However, the circular hut with a conical roof which is constructed by the agricultural peoples of the grasslands offers greater opportunity for architectural creativity. The houses built by the Tiv are an example of this type at its simplest, but of excellent technical quality. The Tiv are renowned as thatchers throughout northern Nigeria. Decoration of the walls may consist of low-relief ornamentation round the doorways, or of painted designs all over the walls.[113] Many of the small 'pagan' tribes of northern Nigeria have exploited mud and stone most effectively in their adaptation of this basic form. Houses are built on a foundation of stones to discourage the penetration of termites into the walls; beds are fashioned in mud to have a space underneath in which a fire can be lit – a veritable hypocaust – to counteract the biting chill of the December and January nights when the Harmattan winds may produce a drop in temperature of as much as 70° F from the day's high.

The houses of the Ham (or Jaba) round Nok afford an outstanding example of the exploitation of the possibilities of mud in architectural design. Their houses are oval in plan with a thatched roof which is nearly vertical over the entrance and slopes more gently to the rear. The small, low doorway leads into a front room, defined by a transverse wall which is pierced by an oval doorway in the centre, giving access to the sleeping quarters behind. These are divided again by a transverse wall which swells out on both sides forming large cavities accessible only from the top of the wall. These are for the storage of grain, not simply where it is protected from rain by the roof of the house, but in an atmosphere kept dry by the fires under the clay beds. The walls over the beds have recesses for the storage of personal property.[114] The Ham have a relatively simple technology, yet they have fully grasped the plastic potential of mud architecture in a way which surpasses that of medieval and later European builders in mud and thatch. European mud architecture often had relief decoration on the wall surface – pargetting – usually done in plaster rather than directly in the mud of the walls. The Ham, however, have produced a house design which is a veritable sculpture for living in, something more than the mere machine for living in which Le Corbusier demanded.

Other peoples in the same area have not incorporated their granaries into the walls of their houses but have made them into independent and beautiful structures. *Ill. 104* shows one. A ring of stones is set in clay to support the granary above the ground to keep termites and rats away. Upon this is set a pre-formed dish of clay, upon which the cylindrical mud walls are built. Apertures are cut in the wall to give access, and the surface round each is decorated in relief. The top is built inwards to a narrow neck just wide enough for a man to get through. The grain is poured in through the lower aperture until that level is reached, when the piece of wall which had been cut out is replaced and sealed in with mud. When the upper aperture is reached the remainder is filled from the top, a lid is sealed in position with clay and a conical roof is set on top to keep off the rain.

In the forests we find rectangular houses with a ridge-pole, a development made possible by the availability of timber. The walls

104 Granary constructed at Jos by a Mada man from Andahar village. The pre-fabricated roof is being raised into position.

105 Ancestor statues, carved door-frame and verandah posts on a completed house similar in style to that in *Ill. 106*. Bafussam chiefdom, of the BaMileke, Cameroun.

of these houses are commonly painted[115] while the BaKuba cover them with decoratively woven matting.[116] In swampy areas houses of this type are built on piles. Sometimes square houses with pyramidal roofs are found in the grasslands. In the Cameroons Grasslands we find a particularly striking example of this development in which the principle of verticality, so important in monumental architecture, is very clearly demonstrated. As can be seen in *Ills. 105* and *106*, the posts (which do not in fact support the roof) afford an opportunity for the sculptor, who also decorates the frame of the door, which is further flanked with the figures of ancestors.[117]

A common type of house in the grasslands of West Africa has a basic structure consisting of a rectangular box of clay with a flat roof which needs wooden reinforcement. The Hausa of northern Nigeria have, since the late nineteenth century, decorated the outer walls of *Ills. 108, 109* these houses with paint or low-relief decoration which may include modern elements such as clocks and bicycles. They use the central rib of a palm frond, *zaure*, to support the flat roof: the useful part of these ribs is limited to a length of ten feet, but by setting them across the corners to reduce the direct span, spans of twenty feet can be achieved. The *zaure* are also used to reinforce the arches in public buildings such as mosques, emir's palaces and town gates.[118] The decoration of the interior of these buildings with relief sculpture and

106 The framework of a square house with pyramidal roof ready for thatching, Bafut, Cameroun.

paint, follows a long-standing tradition. China plates and – nowadays – brightly coloured enamel bowls are set into the walls and ceilings. This mode of decoration appears to have originated on the East African coast where on Kilwa Island Persian and Chinese porcelain bowls were used in this way in the first half of the fifteenth century AD.[119] The practice appears to have spread northwards into Nubia and thence westwards across the Muslim Sudan. It is possible that the Nupe were inspired by this habit in their invention of the fired clay saucer with concentric rills on the convex surface, with which they decorate the walls and floors of some of their houses. These saucers, three to four inches in diameter, are set with the concave side against the moist clay and tapped with a wooden mallet which shatters them and presses the fragments into the clay. The resulting surface is attractive to the eye and resistant to the elements.[120]

This type of architecture has been developed by the peoples of the western Sudan with the sensitivity to its plastic qualities which marked the Ham houses. Round forms have been built, apparently reflecting the round huts. The Dogon of the Niger Bend have rectangular houses and tall tubular granaries of great elegance, and the flat surfaces of the house walls are often relieved with vertical rectangular recesses

Ills. 110, 111

which are also found on the faces of their masks.

The strong African sensitivity to form is shown even in the treatment of the mosque itself, despite the fact that the basic plan is prescribed by Islam. Labelle Prussin has studied the mosques of the Niger Bend and the Volta Basin.[121] Mud buildings here need constant renewal, for although the annual rainfall is not great, it falls during a very short period each year. Permanent wooden scaffolding has been incorporated into the design of the mosques, giving them a prickly appearance. At the same time, however, this provision for frequent repair to the surface appears to have kept even the earliest buildings relatively unchanged in form. The earliest monuments are the San-

Ill. 113

kore Mosque at Timbuktu (reflecting the establishment of Islam as an imperial cult under Mansa Musa of Mali, who flourished from 1312 to 1337) and the tomb of Askia Mohammed at Gao (who ruled Songhay from 1493 to 1529) in essentially the same style – built on a massive scale, with heavy pyramidal forms. Despite its continuing fame Timbuktu never evolved into a stable political centre as did Djenne: it was the stability of this centre which led to the development of skilled craftsmen who created an articulate architecture.

107 Wooden chair, BaMileke, Cameroun. Elaborately carved seats such as this are strictly reserved for chiefs and certain notables. British Museum. Ht 46 in.

108 (*opposite*) The interior of buildings in the Muslim north of Nigeria have been decorated for a long time, but it seems to have been only in the late nineteenth century that the outer walls began to be decorated. In modern Zaria one finds many houses decorated with motifs representing prestige items, in this case a bicycle and a motor car.

109 (*above*) The sculptured surfaces of buildings are often painted, but painted decoration alone is often employed. Zaria, Nigeria.

The mosque at Djenne has an advanced sense of verticality, with hollow minarets integrated into the face of the building. The interior has all the loftiness of a Gothic cathedral. The Mopti Mosque is similar in style and has a sculptural quality which echoes Dogon architecture and masks.

Ills. 110–12

The Djenne and Timbuktu types eventually merge, leading to two other types: those of Bobo Diulasso in Upper Volta and of Kong in Ivory Coast. These result from the southward movement

110 The decorated front of the house of an important person among the Dogon, in the town of Sanga on the bend of the River Niger. (After Griaule.)

111 This Dogon mask, representing *walu* the antelope, was collected at Sạnga and echoes the architectural forms of the Dogon. (After Kjersmeier.) Ht $17\frac{3}{4}$ in.

112 The front of the mosque at Mopti. The resemblance to the face of a Dogon mask is striking. William Fagg suggests that the mask form is copied from that of the mosque, but both seem to have influenced each other. (After Prussin.)

of Muslim Mande traders into these areas, where they established village states. Their mosques reflect the reduction in the scale of the polity, in being smaller and less monumental in style. The moister climate compelled the use of broader buttresses and more liberal horizontal timber scaffolding for the maintenance work, which together reduce the verticality of the design. Indeed, in the Kong type of mosque, the horizontal timbers become so major a feature that the style loses most of its vertical character.

In the small rural mosques, like the one at Kawara, we find that *Ill. 114* sculptural form has taken over completely from architectural form. The result is still very pleasing, but of the two major architectural qualities, horizontality is absent and verticality is minimal. The interior no longer follows the classic plan, indeed it is no longer used,

113 The Sankore mosque at Timbuktu, built in the early fourteenth century. The surface bristles with the permanent wooden scaffolding provided to make possible continuous repair of the building. In consequence the form of the building has remained unchanged since it has never needed to be rebuilt.

126

114 Village mosque at Kawara, Ivory Coast, a late stage in the evolution of the mosque on the Niger Bend.

for the Friday activities are carried out in the open space outside the mosque, as all major African religious ceremonies are.

Thus African creativity has taken over an imported plan and made it entirely its own. Of course, in different parts of Africa, this has been done in different ways. In Ilorin, a Yoruba town in the Kworra State of Nigeria, there are a number of delightful small mosques. *Ill. 118* shows the way in which the sculptural qualities of mud have been exploited in one of them.

In the forests of West Africa, among the Yoruba and the Edo of Benin, a particularly interesting form of building is found, the *impluvium*. Glück regards this as closely related to the clay box house of the savanna, but in structure it is much closer to the usual rectangular ridge-pole house of the forests. Four of these, with verandas, grouped together round a square courtyard could have been the beginning of the development as it clearly was of the Ashanti type of house described by Swithenbank. Among the Yoruba, this is still often all that

Ill. 115

127

115 Traditional decoration of the surface of a mud-built house at Kumasi in Ashanti from a photograph taken by Austin Freeman about 1888, and now in the British Museum.

some *impluvia* consist of, but frequently the courtyard has become quite small, so that the verandas together form a kind of large room with the courtyard reduced to a small open area in the centre into which the rain falls, hence the name, *impluvium* or 'rain courtyard'. Provision is made to catch the water in large pots for storage (nowadays cement-lined tanks are sometimes used) and drains are provided to conduct the water away. In excavations at Ife pavements were found made from sherds of broken pottery set on end which had been the floors of such *impluvia*, with drains at their edge, sometimes a pottery pipe, sometimes a worn-out grindstone pierced by a hole and

Ill. 116

forming a kind of funnel through which the water could pass without eroding the wall.

Impluvia seem no longer to be built in Yorubaland; two-storeyed houses of fired brick or cement block are preferred. Fortunately, however, a number of old houses are still inhabited and maintained. Some of these are palaces, and although Yoruba kings too are building modern houses for themselves, sufficient numbers of traditional ones survive for G.J.A. Ojo to have classified them into four types, each with a different geographical distribution. The Palace in Akure is one of the best-preserved examples, perhaps because the late Deji of Akure, Adesida I, was in his nineties when he died about 1958, and thus was a living embodiment of the traditional way of life. Ojo tells us, for example, that he 'rebuffed finally in 1953 the overtures of some Protestant Churches to build a chapel within the Akure Palace. He considered that it would be a superfluous venture since, as he claimed, there were already seven hundred and twenty deities, each with a temple or shrine of its own in the Palace.'[122] Thanks to his conservatism, the ancient plan of his Palace is still preserved, and one can see that the impluvial courtyards vary from *uwa nla* (the

116 Impluvial courtyard in the palace at Efon Alaye. A modern cement-covered tank now catches the rain which would formerly have been caught in large pots immediately below the eaves. The low wall edging the courtyard confined heavy rains until they could drain away. Note the verandah posts supporting the roof which were carved by Agbonbiofe between 1900 and 1920.

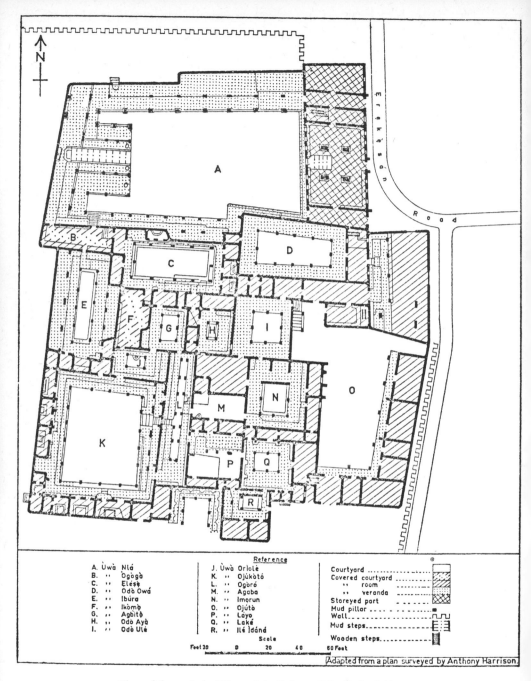

Adapted from a plan surveyed by Anthony Harrison.

117 Plan of the main building of the Palace of the Deji of Akure.

118 One of several small mosques in the northern Yoruba town of Ilorsin. The plastic quality of mud has been very fully exploited.

Great Courtyard, A in *Ill. 117*) with an open area about a hundred and fifty feet long and up to seventy feet wide down to the tiny *uwa odò ayà* (Courtyard of the River Aya, H in the plan) only about nine by four feet.

Ill. 117

In Benin the houses which still survive from the pre-Expedition period, i.e. which date from before 1897, have large numbers of small *impluvia*, which allow adequate light to enter, but not too much heat. The thick mud walls also help to keep the building cool; they are thick enough to accommodate cavities which serve as shelves. Major storage, however, is provided by the completely enclosed rooms which lie beneath the ridge-pole.

Ill. 119

The traditional building method here, as among the Yoruba, consists of puddling the mud with water in a hole in the ground, and

119 Corner of an impluvial room in Chief Oghiamien's house in Benin. The right-hand wall shows the fluting which is permitted on inside walls only to the king and a few high-ranking chiefs. The cavities in the other wall serve as shelves.

when the right consistency has been attained, a continuous course of mud is laid outlining the floor plan of the building, with gaps for the doorways.[123] The Palace of the King of Benin was built with thicker walls than other buildings, with a greater number of courses (seven or more) of mud, and thus a greater height than those of other people's houses. The surfaces of the wall were horizontally fluted. Chiefs' houses were less tall than the Palace (five courses) and also horizontally fluted outside, while a few high-ranking chiefs could have flutings on the interior walls as well, but commoners' houses were limited to four courses and lacked all fluting.[124] The wall surfaces were well smoothed and polished so that the courses of mud are only visible in walls which have been neglected, for a great deal of maintenance is required to repair the effects of rain, not only on the walls themselves but also on the edges of the tank in the floor beneath the *impluvium*. Chief Oghiamien, whose house is a national monument, told me that before Western education was introduced one of the main duties of the children of the house used to be to bring clean 'sand' from the river and to help in restoring the weathered surfaces. Now, however, they are in school most of the time, and it is necessary to pay to have this work done, although there are now relatively few workers trained in this old craft. A new museum has been designed for Benin with an area on the scale and in the style of the King's Palace where works of art intended for the royal cults are to be exhibited, and an area on the scale and in the style of a chief's house for displaying art works of humbler origin. Traditional materials are to be used, with some modernization to inhibit fire, in order to save from extinction the dying craft of wall maintenance. When last heard of, the plan had been blocked by people who considered reinforced concrete to be the perfect material for all buildings.

Probably the best-known architectural monument in the whole of Africa is Zimbabwe in Rhodesia. This spectacular stone ruin has caused more speculation than any other African monument; it has been thought to be King Solomon's Mines, or the Palace of the Queen

120 Zimbabwe. The Temple from the air. The conical tower is in the foreground between the trees.

of Sheba. It was indeed exploited as a mine by the Ancient Ruins Corporation from 1896 to 1901, ransacking the site for ancient gold artefacts to melt down. It has taken the brilliant archaeological excavation of the few tiny undisturbed areas conducted in 1958 by Summers, Robinson, and Whitty to put this site into its proper chronological setting.

Ill. 120 There are three main groups of buildings at Zimbabwe. In the valley is the elliptical building or 'temple', which has a massive outer wall thirty feet high and twenty thick, enclosing another smaller incomplete wall, a tall conical tower, a smaller tower and a mass of fallen stonework from other buildings. This was apparently the Royal Palace, and since the Monomotapa who reigned here was a divine king, it was also in some sense a temple. About a quarter of a mile to the north is a granite hill, which is precipitously steep on the east side. Stone walls and terraces have been constructed between the boulders on the hill to make a fortification; access is by a stepped pathway. Although this site is known as the 'acropolis', it clearly served as a place of refuge, comparable to the keep in a Norman castle. Between these two groups of buildings are the valley ruins, a complex mass of walling and enclosures.

The excavations revealed that the site was occupied before the stone buildings were erected. The earliest traces of occupation seem to belong to the second and third centuries A D while the second phase, equated with the proto-MaKaranga, is recognized in the remains of round huts built of poles plastered with clay, and containing pottery figurines of cattle. This phase of occupation began about A D 330. It is not known when it ended, but there is a gap in the archaeological record before the third phase, from A D 1085 to 1450, the proto-MaShona occupation, which saw the beginnings of stone building. The defensive hill-top acropolis was probably resorted to as a refuge in its natural state, and some of the earliest stone buildings are found there, conceived as extensions of the natural rock, rather than as independent walls. Mortarless dry stone walling was used to fill in the gaps between the boulders. Eventually, the idea of building true free-standing walls was conceived. When these walls join at an angle they are not keyed into each other as stone or brick walls usually are, but they simply abut each other, like mud walls. This suggests very strongly that the technique of building with stone evolved on the spot. Four different types of wall construction have

134

béen distinguished by Anthony Whitty, all of them consisting of a roughly dressed stone facing with a rubble core. Class P is moderately neatly built, but without courses; Class PQ is intermediate between this and Class Q which is well built with neat courses; Class R is rough, uncoursed and poorly built. The analysis of wall junctions on the Great Enclosure shows that this scheme represents a chronological sequence there. The same styles are found in the other buildings on the site, so that it has been possible to work out the sequence of building in broad terms.

121 Decorative stone walling at Naletale, apparently built by the BaRozwi in the seventeenth and eighteenth centuries.

Class P walls are related only to the basic constructional needs, but Class PQ sees the introduction of architectural considerations such as buttressed entrances and rounded wall ends. The culmination of this development in Class Q walls produced the finest buildings and the neatest work. This level of skill was reached in the later part of the fourth phase, during the BaRozwi occupation, from AD 1450 to 1833, and culminated in the Great Wall of the Enclosure, the Conical Tower and the Platform. This phase occurred at the peak of Zimbabwe's prosperity, reflected in the quantities of gold which were mined here by the Ancient Ruins Corporation. The Class R walls belong to the fifth phase of occupation, the time of the Mugabe occupation, from 1833, when the Nguni sacked Zimbabwe, until the end of the nineteenth century, during which time the Great Enclosure served merely as a cattle kraal.

Ill. 121

Zimbabwe is by no means the only group of stone buildings in southern Africa. The Khami Ruins are hardly less impressive, and Naletale in Rhodesia, which was occupied by the BaRozwi in the seventeenth and eighteenth centuries, has outstandingly fine decorative walling. Ruins of stone buildings are scattered throughout Rhodesia from the Limpopo to the Zambezi, and throughout the Inyanga Mountains on the eastern border of Rhodesia. These are all complexes of circular buildings, no doubt deriving their form from prototypes in mud. It seems probable that the idea of building in stone arose from the need to terrace the hillsides for cultivation and to make platforms for houses. Indeed, further north at Engaruka in Tanzania, there are such retaining walls with circles of stone which seem to be the floors of huts. Some of the few radiocarbon dates so far obtained[125] suggest that these are in part earlier than the stone constructions at Zimbabwe, and that they may represent the basic form of the traditions which were to bloom at Zimbabwe from the fifteenth century onwards. By this time the Indian Ocean trade was well established and it may be that the exotic influences, perhaps by raising the level of available wealth, encouraged the undertaking of such public buildings in stone on a truly monumental scale. Certainly, Zimbabwe would hardly have been possible without the wealth which the trade in gold and copper made possible. Nevertheless, the groups of circular forms of the Zimbabwe buildings are similar in arrangement to the buildings of the Palace of the Paramount Chief of Barotseland, which is built of reeds and wooden poles.

122 Fragment of a wall built from sun-dried bricks decoratively laid. This technique may well be the antecedent of decorative building with stone, for stone architecture in Africa seems always to copy mud prototypes. This example is in the abandoned town of Old Somorika in Afenmai, north-east of Benin. The stone benches were provided for the comfort of the elders, for this is the edge of the meeting area in the centre of the town.

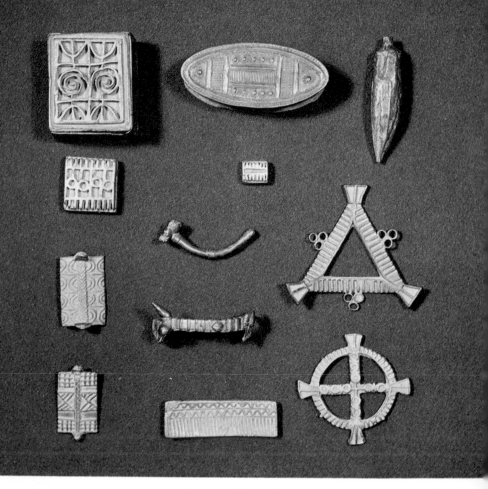

123 Brass weights for measuring gold-dust which was the currency of Ashanti. Many of them refer to proverbial expressions. *Left* (top to bottom): cast box for storing gold-dust: the double spiral motif is a sign of creation by the supreme being; weight with a geometric design edged with the life-giving rays of the sun; two shields: 'when a shield wears out the framework still remains', i.e. men die but their deeds live on. *Centre*: a repoussé storage box; a small geometric weight; a war-trumpet decorated with human jaws: 'when a horn merits a jawbone one is added to it', i.e. rewards have to be earned; a cartridge-belt: 'the cartridge belt of Akowua [a celebrated warrior] has never been known to lack bullets', i.e. a resourceful person is never found wanting; a geometric design representing the fire of the sun. *Right*: a weight cast directly from a real okra fruit: 'the okra does not show its seeds through its skin', i.e. there is more in a man's mind than shows on his face; a triangular weight representing the sky, the earth and the underworld symbol of Nyame as ruler of the universe; an equal-armed cross edged with the sun's rays, symbol of Nyame as the sun god. Coll. F. Willett. The okra measures $2\frac{3}{4}$ in.

138

CHAPTER FIVE

Looking at African Sculpture

The first step towards appreciating any art is, of course, to look at it. We have the writings of many artists and critics to help us to look at and to enjoy African sculpture in particular. Yet they are in some respects fallible guides, for they start from the premise of Western ideas of beauty and all too often express themselves ethnocentrically, as when Margaret Trowell writes of the BaYaka and BaPende as having 'elaborate masks of the scarecrow variety'.[126] Her entire assessment of the art of the Ashanti is that it has 'little to commend it as of serious interest. The ingenious little goldweights, although pleasing in their wealth of representation of local proverbs, must be relegated to the class of collector's trifles, while the small fertility figures known as *Akua Mma* with their curious plate-like heads are of more real interest to the ethnologist than to the artist.'[127] This has certainly not been my own experience: both artists and art students whom I have introduced to Ashanti gold weights and dolls have found them exciting. This then is the problem. Is it sufficient to look at, and either to like or to dislike, a particular African sculpture or art style?

Ill. 123

Ill. 101

As Wingert put it, 'For the art historian and for the serious art connoisseur or collector, this art has certainly very important advantages over the study of other traditions. For one thing there is not the vast bulk of historical and analytical literature, so that it is possible for the individual to exercise his own powers of perception and analysis without any fixed attitude to direct or curtail his observations. In other words, when dealing with primitive art, the scholar and the art connoisseur can with all freedom express their own aesthetic interpretations and judgments.'[128] Surely it is only the professional art historian who may be inhibited from exercising his own

124, 125 Collectors have often attempted to estimate the age of African sculpture by its appearance. Despite the differences in condition, these two figures with movable lower jaws operated by a rod which passes vertically through the trunk, were found together in a hut during a punitive expedition among the Ogoni near Opobo, Nigeria, in 1913. Manchester Museum. Hts shown $18\frac{1}{4}$, $17\frac{3}{4}$ in.

127 Male figure carved by the Mama who make the bush-cow masks seen in *Ill. 128*. Their purpose is not known. British Museum. Ht $26\frac{3}{8}$ in.

126 Mask representing a bush pig. Ogoni. The movable lower jaw and cane teeth are greatly favoured by the Ogoni, though they are used also by neighbouring Ibibio. British Museum. L. $16\frac{1}{4}$ in.

128, 129 Without documentation in the field the subject of a sculpture may not always be identified with certainty. The headpiece for the *mangam* ceremonies of the Mama has retained the characteristic horns of the bush-cow despite the simplification of the form. Nigerian Museum, Lagos. L. $19\frac{1}{2}$ in. The Jukun headpiece however is an extreme stylization of the human head, the projection at the back representing the tuft of hair left on the otherwise shaven heads of Jukun men, while that at the front is said to be the nose. This piece was collected by Frobenius in 1912. It is called *aku onu* and is used in the *akumaga* cult to represent a beneficent spirit who speaks for the ancestors on occasions when good fortune is celebrated, and at funerals. Museum für Völkerkunde, Berlin. Ht 10 in., L. 19 in.

130 The Ogoni show a great liking for masks with movable jaws, some of which, like this one representing an elephant, appear to be intended to amuse the spectator. British Museum. L. $18\frac{1}{2}$ in.

141

powers of perception and analysis by 'the vast bulk of historical and analytical literature'. Most visitors to exhibitions of Western art, ancient or modern, are able to enjoy themselves to a certain degree without necessarily having read all the relevant monographs. Yet to gain the maximum appreciation, a knowledge, for example, of which artists preceded and influenced others, deepens both one's understanding and one's enjoyment. In this respect African art is no different from Western art; the greater the knowledge, the greater the enjoyment.

131 This mother with child by an Afo sculptor is among the finest treatments of the theme in the whole of Africa. It is thought to represent a female ancestor, the mother of the Afo people, for a similar piece is still in use in her shrine. The fact that the baby at her breast has herself mature breasts suggests that this is more than just an ordinary mother and child. Although few in numbers, the Afo enjoyed a high reputation as artists among neighbouring peoples, though their finest works seem to date from before 1900. Horniman Museum, London. Ht $27\frac{1}{2}$ in.

132 A British District Officer on tour in the Nigerian Creeks, represented by Thomas Ona who used a traditional Yoruba style to represent everyday life around him, both European and African. Europeans, not accustomed to seeing themselves represented in an African style of sculpture presumed that they were being caricatured. Ona however declared, when interviewed by William Bascom, that he was simply representing the world as he saw it. The group is constructed from many parts, even the D.O.'s hat and pipe are separate carvings. Coll. R.P. Armstrong. L. 16¼ in.

A great deal of satisfaction can indeed be found in looking at African sculpture without background information, looking simply to see how the artist has solved his artistic problems, but one is not necessarily sharing in the sculptor's experience or enjoying the sensations he intended to convey. One can observe first of all the overall artistic conception in terms of masses and open space. The use of open space enclosed within sculptures by African artists appears as one of the more obvious features borrowed by twentieth-century Western sculptors. Depending on the degree of emphasis on the masses and the open spaces the impression may be of weight or of lightness, which may reflect the function of the sculpture, but the measure of the sculptor's success in this cannot be gauged without knowledge of his purpose.

143

133 Profile of Yoruba *ibeji* (figure of a twin) in the style of the city of Oyo.

African sculpture has been commonly described as frontal, i.e. the figures are symmetrically disposed about a vertical axis, and face forward. There are, of course, exceptions to this, but asymmetrical pieces are uncommon. Because of their frontality African figure sculptures are commonly photographed or drawn full face, concealing the fact that the sculptor has paid a great deal of attention to the profile view. Female twin figures (*ibeji*) in the Oyo style very often show a remarkable balance between the breasts and the buttocks which is only apparent in profile.

Ill. 133

It is easy enough to analyse the formal characteristics of African sculpture in terms of vertical, horizontal or diagonal emphases; of relative naturalism or abstraction; of rounded, angular or cubic elements; or in terms of tensions, rhythm and movement, and this is certainly an enjoyable and satisfying experience, since African sculptors have achieved a remarkable level of expression in what has been called 'purely sculptural' form.

Ills. 134–35

Western artists of the present century were very quick to appreciate this, once the camera had made academic naturalism a superfluous ideal in two-dimensional art. They saw what they took to be free creative interpretations of nature, totally unrestricted by the canons of realism, and saw how their own art could be freed. They were, in fact, mistaken in believing that there were no bounds for the individual artist, and as more African sculptures were brought to Europe, it rapidly became clear that their creators were working within an artistic tradition which had developed over many centuries.

144

It is perfectly reasonable to look at African sculpture through Western eyes. The painter Fred Uhlman has described his own approach to collecting African art. 'I bought my first African mask . . . not because I liked it but because I felt that being now a painter I had to be in the movement. Most of the artists I admired, Picasso, Modigliani, Derain, to mention only a few, had collected African art and had been profoundly influenced by it. Shortly afterwards I bought the Baule fetish and the Baule bobbin which are still two of the finest pieces in my collection. It is easy to see why I bought them and why from that moment I have never stopped collecting. The head of the bobbin or heddle-pulley which is after all only a functional object for the purpose of weaving seemed to me then and today as beautiful as a Greek goddess. The fetish moved me as deeply as the bobbin by its silent tragic dignity and its air of profound meditation. They

134, 135 Two figures of horsemen from the Senufo, fine examples of the 'purely sculptural form' which artists and critics admire in African art. They represent two of the *bandeguele*, minor divinities concerned with divination. British Museum. Hts 12¾, 10 in

appealed to me as a *European* brought up in the classic tradition of Greece and Rome. Everything I have ever bought is submitted to the same test: does it speak to me and does it move me.

'Somebody may argue that this is too narrow an approach and that it means that I exclude works of great power. This may be so but for me it is the only honest and reasonable approach if one collects for *pleasure* and not because something is strange or rare or a good investment. After all I have to *live* with my collection.'[129]

I have met many collectors who began in a similar way, buying a single piece, often on the spur of the moment, and, as they lived with it, being seduced by its aesthetic quality into collecting more and more examples of African sculpture.

This approach to African art, enjoying it for what it communicates immediately, is a valid one. It could be argued that the reaction to a work of art is a creative act which is the counterpart of the action of the artist. There can be no question that African sculpture moves Western viewers, and that its effect increases with further exposure. Yet at this level of study understanding is limited in much the same way as it is in the study of prehistoric art. The scenes of pastoral life represented in the Tassili can be easily enjoyed, but one can only guess at the artists' motivation.

Fred Uhlman's account shows that he appreciates that his approach is one of communication between the art and himself; he does not assume that he is thereby communicating with the original artist. Some writers, however, in adopting a similar subjective approach, asking 'What does this sculpture mean to me?' have presumed that the meaning they extract from a sculpture is the meaning which the artist intended to convey. Leon Underwood, as one of the rare European sculptors who himself carries out the entire process of casting his bronze sculptures, has thrown great light on the technical aspects of ancient bronze castings[130] yet when he writes about wood carvings he sometimes suggests that his own interpretation is that of the original artist: 'In this figure [a woman with a large head, cupping her breasts in her hands, but without a child] woman is represented in her biological role – human fertility; whereas [a figure with a small head, nursing a child] . . . personifies, with her child *mankind*, a more comprehensive idea of fertility – that of the earth. The association of the idea of woman as mother of the race with mother of the universe (the earth of Africa) is emphasized in sculptural expressions

146

136 Some of the first African sculpture to be sought out by European collectors was that produced by the Baule. The high polish, the careful representation of exotic details of hair-style and scarification pattern together with the serenity of expression appealed immediately to European taste. This figure of an ancestor is typical of Baule sculpture. British Museum. Ht 20½ in.

137 Three figures from northern Nigeria. The one on the left appears to have been used by the Chamba but may have been made by a Mumuye, while the other two are certainly Mumuye. A remarkable feature of the style is the way in which the arms and even the abdomen of one piece are used to enclose space within the sculpture. *Left* and *centre*: British Museum. *Right*: formerly Coll. James Crabtree. Hts $18\frac{3}{4}$, $18\frac{3}{8}$, $17\frac{1}{2}$ in.

by a reduction of the head, thereby giving a monumental scale to the body.'[131]

In describing an Urhobo piece similar to *Ill. 138* he is less assured and indicates some but not all of his own interpretations by questions: 'The fanged maw and legs of the animal at the base are those of the leopard. The leopard's head is reduced to a fanged mouth, mounted directly without body on legs. The legs are painted with leopard's spots. Does it mean ferocious speed or swift ferocity? The head of the divinity or spirit in the centre is attended on each side by baboon-like figures with human-faced birds (messengers?) on their heads. . . .'[132] The author's subjective interpretation, however, permeates the passage; for example spots of paint by no means necessarily represent the leopard, as in *Ill. 234*.

148

138 Two *ejiri* of the Western Ijo representing the head of the household making sacrifice to the family guardian spirit represented below as a strange animal, commonly said to be an elephant, though the trunk appears never to be represented. The creature is probably entirely imaginary. The Urhobo also have similar sculptures. British Museum. Hts 32¼, 27½ in.

139 Senufo mask called *kponiugo* representing a mythical being who protects the community from sorcerers and soul-stealers. He is represented with the jaws of a hyena, the tusks of a wart-hog, the horns of an antelope and of some other creature. Appropriately the mask is intended to recall the chaos before the world was set in order. Between the horns are a hornbill and a chameleon, two of the primordial animals. The chameleon's slow and careful walk is due to the fact that he was the first creature to walk on the newly formed surface of the earth. These masks appear in groups after dark and appear to spit fire, for tinder is held in a cleft stick in front of the mouth. Courtesy of the Art Institute of Chicago. L. 40$\frac{1}{8}$ in.

Writers about the arts of the Western world pay heed not just to the formal qualities of a work of art, but to its date and place of composition, the patron, the purpose and the meaning. The meaning not infrequently reflects ideas with which the reader may be presumed to be relatively familiar, events in the life of Christ or the lives of the saints, famous historical events or personages. If this background information should relate to an obscure event or person, the art historian usually provides the necessary information. So much of the background is familiar that it is often taken for granted, and in consequence, since it is not formally expressed, it is often forgotten that this knowledge is a vital part of our appreciation of a work of art. Hence, many writers trained in art history seem to believe that it is possible to appreciate the arts of the non-Western world without any knowledge of the world of ideas which they reflect.

140, 141 Wooden bowl for holding the sixteen palm nuts used in Ifa divination. The man on horseback is a favourite subject for supporting this type of Yoruba bowl. British Museum. Ht 11¼ in.

142, 143 Wooden bowl for the cult of the Yoruba god Obatala, whose *igbin* drums are represented being played by women. Nigerian Museum, Lagos. Ht 10½ in.

While it is clearly possible to get some enjoyment out of a work of art of any period without knowledge of the circumstances in which it was created, we need to have this information for the maximum enjoyment, which only true understanding can bring. When we look at sculpture we ask what the artist was trying to do; without specialized information we cannot know whether he is attempting to represent the spirit of an ancestor, a chief, a worshipper or even a god. Similarly, what determines the scale of the work? Is it intended to be placed in a dominant static position or is it intended to be portable? This is not always clear from the object itself, for William Fagg and I were shown a sculpture in a shrine in northern Ekiti which was over six feet high and weighed at least a hundred and twenty pounds – yet it was intended for wear on the head as an *epa* mask.

African sculptures show a variety of styles ranging from naturalism to the most abstract stylization. Without additional information it is quite impossible to guess the meaning of the more stylized works. Most African sculpture in Western collections is unpainted, yet in Africa sculpture is probably more commonly painted than not. How can we then assess the surface finish of a sculpture if we do not know whether or not it was intended to be visible?

The most treacherous ground of all, however, is that of the mood or expression of a sculpture. Western writers are very prone to look for expressions of horror and terror in African masks which in their own society may be intended merely to amuse.

A very strong influence in writings about African art has been the collector, whether private or public, i.e. the museum curator. Rarity and especially uniqueness have been set up as supreme values. We see many exhibitions of 'masterpieces of African art,' albeit most of these include very pedestrian works. Even where the works are carefully selected with an encyclopaedic knowledge of the field, as for example in the exhibition organized by William Fagg 'Africa: 100 Tribes – 100 Masterpieces',[133] one may well ask how a masterpiece can be typical or how a single work of whatever quality can represent a whole people. We can hardly write an adequate art history in the terms of masterpieces alone, for we need to study the whole range of artistic production in order to detect the outstanding achievements. Advances, on the whole, have been made by the outstanding individual artists in each generation who have resolved problems more effectively than their contemporaries, so that when

152

144 Pottery tobacco pipe showing the exaggerated nose which is typical of BaYaka sculpture. This form may have been developed from the upturned nose of BaPende sculptures (*Ills. 188, 189*), while the large fleshy nose of other Ba-Yaka sculptures is an exaggeration of a more naturalistic form. Both look amusing to European eyes, but we cannot be certain that this is their effect on a MuYaka. Manchester Museum. Ht $2\frac{13}{16}$ in

we read a book on art history we usually read only about the more gifted and influential 'great' masters. Yet we cannot appreciate the achievements of the great masters without a knowledge of the lesser ones. The true masterpieces must be studied in the context of the overall artistic production of the society.

Despite this emphasis on the 'masterpiece,' those who approach African art from a purely aesthetic point of view seem until recently not to have regarded the artist as having any real individuality. It was considered important to determine the origin of the piece – a tribal name was usually enough – but the name of the individual artist was not usually sought since it was felt that the tribe as a whole in some vague way produced the style, that the artist was merely expressing with greater or lesser skill the aesthetic conceptions of the tribe. In fact, there are two forces at work in the creation of traditional African sculpture: the established artistic style appropriate to the type of object being made, and the individual vision of the carver himself. The more able and sensitive the sculptor, the greater the individuality of his work.

145 BaYaka dance mask showing an extreme development of the trumpet-ended nose. After circumcision, which is the culmination of the segregation in the bush school (*nkanda*), the boys dance in masks like this in all the villages of their district. There is no secrecy about the identity of the dancers, who receive prizes for their skill, while the carver is honoured for his originality. The face of these masks is commonly set in a frame while the superstructure is made of raffia fibre and usually represents an animal. Rietberg Museum, Zürich. Ht 21¼ in.

146 The initiation masks of the BaSuku are related to those of the BaYaka, but are entirely carved in wood, including the superstructure. The nose lacks the BaYaka exaggeration. Rietberg Museum, Zürich. Ht 23½ in.

So long as African art was studied primarily in the museums and armchairs of the West, so long was it possible for the myth of the anonymity of the carver to persist, for it was only on the soil of Africa that one could discover the names of individual artists. Although anthropologists had long been undertaking field-work in Africa, they had somehow not paid much heed to the art, and when they did, they were apt to make some surprising comments. 'The art of woodcarving is governed in part by the poor quality of the tools, the blades and cutting-edges of which are ineffective when faced by a hard and unyielding substance. Further, the sculptor who practises the "direct" method of carving, with neither a design nor a ground plan of the work in progress, works by trial and error: he requires, therefore a material which is . . . easily cut, one that lends itself to experiment and correction.'[134] Practically every part of this statement is untrue. While traditionally-wrought iron was soft, it took a very sharp edge and is commonly said to have been far more efficient than the cutting tools now made locally from imported steel tempered for other purposes (for example matchets and knives are commonly made nowadays from motor-car springs), but however good or bad the tools, carvings of very high quality were made in the hardest woods, such as *iroko*, which indeed had to be carved when freshly felled before they reached maximum hardness. While it is true that African artists work directly, without preliminary sketches, they do have a remarkable vision of the end-product from the time of making the first cut. It is an amazing experience to see a carver cut an elaborate interlace design covering a large panel without ever having to change a line, or modify the size of one section of the design to make the whole fit in. By the end of his apprenticeship, an African artist has achieved the motor skills to match his vision. Father Carroll tells us: 'No matter how complicated a work may be and though he has no drawing to guide him, Bandele never cuts away by accident any wood he may need later; he would be ashamed to have to add another piece.'[135] The only Yoruba sculpture I know in which the carver evidently made an error in cutting is the work of an apprentice. Of course, there are circumstances in which carvings – usually masks – are made by the initiate who has not been apprenticed. This is commonly the case for example among the Dogon, whose

Ill. 111 masks are carved of very soft wood. Here is another instance of the dangers of generalization about African art; here the tendency is

156

to judge African art as a whole on the basis of one particular group closely studied by the writer. Such generalizations among French writers are often based on familiarity with the Dogon. Let me candidly warn the reader that I myself, though I try consciously to avoid it, may tend to generalize on a basis of Yoruba practices.

African art has a great appeal, more intense and more widespread than ever before. Why is this? For one thing, the break with naturalism in Western art, which was so indebted to the artists' discovery of African art has made us all more receptive to the stylized forms of African sculpture. Within the corpus of African art styles there is such a great variety that there is something for every taste. Even Op Art was anticipated by the BaSongye in their masks. The principal *Ill. 147* reason for studying African art, however, is the reason we study any art: because it is one of the highest expressions of human culture, which can bring us continual refreshment – re-creation in its strictest sense. The fact that it has so much to offer to students of art in the West shows its importance as part of the artistic heritage of the whole of mankind. The peoples of the new nations of Africa take pride in this for it provides them, as it does Americans of African descent, with one of their best hopes for acceptance by the world at large as equals both as nations and as individuals.

147 Mask from the BaSongye, whose word for mask, *kifwebe*, is commonly applied by collectors to this type of mask. Some of these masks appear to represent spirits of the ancestors during initiation ceremonies. Musée Royal de l'Afrique Centrale, Tervuren. Ht 22 in.

148 BaLuba mask the decoration of which appears to be derived from the BaSongye. Used in ceremonies associated with chieftaincy. Musée Royal de l'Afrique Centrale, Tervuren. Ht 23¾ in.

149 Helmet mask used in boys' initiation rites of the Northern BaKete who live among the BaKuba. Coll. Jay T. Last. Ht 21 in.

150, 151, 152 Wooden figures collected by Robert Hottot among the BaFumu section of the BaTeke in 1906. The one on the left has had its magical substance (*bonga*) removed and is called a *tege*. The other figures with their *bonga*, which is the effective source of their power, are called *butti*. The power of the fetish is said to be specific: success in hunting or trading; protection against disease. Their power comes ultimately from the ancestors for the *bonga* contains such material as hair from the head of a venerated elder and white chalk, symbol of the bones of the ancestors. British Museum. Ht $6\frac{3}{4}$, 5 and $5\frac{3}{4}$ in.

CHAPTER SIX

Understanding African Sculpture

It is important for us not to deceive ourselves into believing that we can understand the intention of an African sculptor simply by looking at his work. For a true understanding we have to study African art and artists on the soil of Africa, or, if we cannot do this for ourselves, then we should pay particular attention to the studies which are based on direct observation in the field. Studies in the field have frequently disproved generalizations formulated by scholars in their museums and studies, and in doing so have sometimes produced new concepts. It has been found, for example, that although sculpture in Africa is very commonly painted, the paint is often applied without any reference to the sculptural form. In the case of the masks made by the Kalabari of the Niger Delta, Horton has discovered that this is because the painting is not simply an enrichment of the sculpture, but is the means whereby the spirit is brought to occupy the mask.[136]

THE PROPORTIONS OF THE BODY

A feature of African sculpture which has intrigued scholars from the first is that the head is commonly represented as disproportionately large. For a long time, this was thought to be a childlike characteristic, a result of the carver's paying too much attention to the details, instead of to the overall proportions.[137] Field-studies, however, from many parts of Africa have shown that sculptors begin by dividing up the block of wood very carefully into separate parts which will eventually be the head, body and legs. The proportions are thus deliberately established at the outset and are certainly not due to lack of skill. The first person to observe this was a French doctor, Robert Hottot, travelling among the BaTeke on the Lower Congo as early as 1906; unfortunately his most valuable observations were not published until after his death.[138]

Ills. 150–52

153 Wooden figure (*bieri*) from a reliquary of ancestors' bones of the Fang. The proportions of an infant together with signs of physical maturity, reflect the continuity of the life cycle, for the newborn has come from the ancestors. Coll. Arman. Ht $18\frac{1}{8}$ in.

Ill. 153   More recently James Fernandez has discovered the meaning that these proportions have for the Fang of Gabon, where they occur in figures which stand on the boxes containing the ancestors' bones. He points out that 'the large torso, the big head, and the flexed, disproportionately small legs are definitely infantile in character. Now . . . the statue presents both an infantile and an ancestral aspect. While the Fang argue that the statues represent age, the ancestors, and their august powers in their descendants' affairs, they also recognize the infantile qualities of the figures themselves.' He explains that these contradictory qualities imply cosmological and theological explanations. '. . . the newborn are felt to be especially close to the ancestors and are only gradually weaned away by ritual and time to human status. Another explanation . . . lies in the primary concern of the ancestral cult in fertility and increase. An infantile representation is an apt expression of the desire for children . . . these contradictory qualities in the ancestor figure give it a vitality for the Fang that it would not possess if it simply figured an aged person or an infant.'[139]

162

154 Masked figure accompanied by musicians, Baule. Groupings of figures like this have long been made on top of *kuduo* by the related Ashanti, and the individual figures are similar to gold weights made by both peoples. This piece was probably made for Baule use for its quality seems to be too good for tourist art. Coll. F. Willett. Ht 4⅞ in.

Similar ideas may have led to the production of a terracotta head of the Nok culture found at Wamba in which the form of the head is infantile although the face is bearded.

Ill. 156

THE FUNCTION OF ART IN AFRICAN SOCIETY

It has commonly been asserted that there is no 'art for art's sake' in Africa, and also that all African art is religious. In Western society, when art critics speak of 'art for art's sake', they mean that the artist produces an object which is valued for itself, which attempts neither to instruct nor to edify, a product in which the artist is concerned exclusively with the solution of artistic problems of composition, colour or form. The content of the work of art is secondary to these considerations. The final product, however, does have an acquired social function – it may be used to decorate a room or serve as a status symbol. Now this academic attitude to art appears to be of quite recent origin. At one time all European art had a social purpose – whether to instruct the faithful, to edify the devout, or to commemorate the noble. Traditional African art similarly has its social purposes, but there are some products whose purpose is not clearly defined. The Fon of Dahomey, for example, make brass castings of animals and of people at work or in processions, which have no religious or didactic intent. They are made as objects of beauty by the brass-smith

155 Mask of the type shown in *Ill. 154*. It is said to represent an antelope. Himmelheber 1960, Plate 156a to f shows two of these masks in action in a musical performance. British Museum. L. 33 in.

156 Terracotta head of the Nok culture found in tin-mining at Wamba. The form of the head is infantile yet it has a moustache and beard. Jos Museum. Ht $5\frac{1}{2}$ in.

and in this respect are to be considered examples of 'art for art's sake'. Yet they do have a social function which is entirely independent of the subject represented; that of establishing prestige, brass being regarded as a semi-precious metal; only the wealthy can afford to buy them, and they are displayed in the home both as objects of beauty and as status symbols.[140] Himmelheber found the *Ill. 157* Dan produce *objets d'art* for mere aesthetic enjoyment, but only in brass. Such an object is placed near the fire where the entering guest sees it at his first glance. "These objects may be little animals, or a man and his wife with all sorts of characteristic attributes as gun, basket, pipe."[141] The fine Baule brass casting of a figure wearing an *Ill. 154* antelope mask, and surrounded by musicians probably functioned in a similar way as an artistic status symbol. Kenneth Murray has mentioned a young carver in the Ilaje area of western Yorubaland who had covered his walls with combs and spoons of various designs as a decoration.[142]

157 Bronze figure of a man hoeing, from the Fon, among whom they serve as objects of prestige, either to own or to give as presents, for bronze is regarded as a valuable metal and according to Herskovits the castings are looked upon as jewels. The craft has of late become directed chiefly towards the tourist trade. Manchester Museum. Ht $3\frac{13}{16}$ in.

Similarly, it is not true that all African art is religious. Adrian Gerbrands[143] has demonstrated this very clearly, using the documented pot lids collected among the BaWoyo of Cabinda, just north of the mouth of the Congo River, by two missionary Fathers, brothers named Jan and Frans Vissers. It is the custom among these people for the husband to eat separately from his wife. When the wife has a disagreement with her husband, she covers his food with a wooden lid sculptured with figures which convey through the proverbial expressions they symbolize, the substance of her dissatisfaction. Of course, the wife chooses an occasion when her husband is entertaining his friends, so that they, representing the community at large, can arbitrate. She usually receives a number of these lids from her mother and mother-in-law when she marries, but if she does not possess one appropriate to her problem, she gets one made.

158 BaWoyo proverb pot-lid from the village of Monaquena, Cabinda. The woman lying in the centre beating her head on the ground like a frightened lizard is imploring her husband's pity. At her feet the shell *nsosse* indicates 'I am going to tell you what is on my mind.' The three cooking stones are scattered round the edge of the lid: normally they stand close together to support the cooking pot on the fire; since the pot will fall if one is removed, they indicate that 'all good things come in threes', i.e. in marriage the husband must give his wife clothes; the wife must look after the cooking; and there must be children. The general import is that something is wrong with the marriage and the wife begs the husband's pity in putting it right. Rijksmuseum voor Volkenkunde, Leiden. Diam. $6\frac{3}{4}$ in.

159 *Malongo* fetish figure from the BaKongo. The fetish material on the abdomen is covered with an imported mirror, while more of it has been moulded into a hat. The eyes are covered with glass. The upraised right hand formerly held a weapon. This piece was already in a museum collection by 1897. Manchester Museum. Ht $10\frac{5}{8}$ in.

The lids vary in complexity. One shows a round pot supported on three stones. With fewer than three stones the pot would fall over, hence it signifies the proverb: 'All good things come in threes,' i.e. a husband must give his wife clothes; a wife must cook for her husband; there must be children. The lid, therefore, is a general indication that there is something lacking in the marriage. The husband himself will know what it is.

Ill. 158

167

In some cases the lid is decorated with a large number of objects including audiovisual puns: such as the *conus* shell which is called *nsosse*, which sounds like a sucked-in sound of annoyance, and hence means 'I am angry and I am going to tell you why'; or another shell called *zinga*, a word which also means 'life', and hence family life, harmony, and thus conveys the exhortation to 'live in harmony with your family'. Clearly this is purely secular art and this single example vividly disproves the assertion that all African art is religious. Many other examples could be found. Among the Yoruba for instance it is the custom to offer kola nuts to visitors: a wealthy man would offer them in an elaborately carved lidded bowl kept specially for the purpose. The most elaborate ones represent a woman kneeling with a cock in her hands.

Nevertheless, it is true that a great deal of African art has a religious purpose, yet even within the field of religious sculpture there is a great variety of practices. It is usual for the act of carving itself to be hedged round with rituals, since the tree which provides the wood is generally regarded as the home of a spirit which needs to be placated. In the case of sculptures which are to be a home for a spirit, such as the masks and ancestor figures of the Dogon, it is easy to see that a conflict between the two forces inhabiting the wood needs to be avoided. Among the Dogon the life force of the tree is controlled by driving little iron hooks into the mask, since the life force of the iron is more powerful than that of the wood. Yet even where no later spirit occupation is involved, as in Yoruba drums, and even in the case of secular objects like stools, the spirit of the tree still needs to be propitiated.

It is sometimes surprising, therefore, to find that old carvings are commonly neglected. This is especially true of masks which are usually occupied by the spirit only during the ceremonies; between times they are regarded as so much wood. In the case of some Dogon masks, new ones are used once and then abandoned to decay, though as a result of increasing Western contact, they are commonly re-covered for sale to collectors, who set their own special value on decay as an index of age and authenticity! Other types of carving too may be abandoned if they cease to function properly. Hottot observed that the fetish[144] figures of the BaTeke could be deconsecrated by removing the medicine from the abdominal socket; the priest who does this would keep the figure by him and later supply it with fresh

160 Fetish figures of the BaBembe have the 'medicine' hidden inside the trunk through a hole between the legs. BaBembe sculptures are usually small in size with cicatrices carefully represented on the trunk. British Museum. Ht 10¼ in.

medicine for another client. The BaTeke distinguish clearly between such a figure when it is endowed with medicine which they call *butti*, and one which has not received the medicine, or from which it has been removed, which they call *tege*.

Ills. 150–52

AFRICAN SCULPTURE IN ITS SETTING
In the West we think of art as meant to be openly and continuously on view, but some African sculptures are seen only by a select band of initiates. An example is the figure in *Ill. 162*, which was seen only by initiates of the Ogboni Society, who were involved in the cult of the earth and also formed a major political force among the Yoruba.[145] Some shrine figures are not seen by devotees, only by the priests of the cult. In contrast Chief Obaloran, who is in charge of the Orisha Iko cult in Ife, is not permitted to see the terracotta sculpture

Ill. 161

Ills. 68, 233

which is used in the festival, though other worshippers may. Sometimes sculptures of a more common kind, such as the twin figures of the Yoruba, wear special clothes or wrappings which partly hide them from view when they stand on family shrines. When Hottot wished to photograph a fetish figure among the BaTeke in 1906, he took it outside the owner's hut. 'The figure was clothed in ample red robes, fixed at the neck. . . . We removed its . . . garments, to get a photograph of the carving. Having taken my photograph I realized that the village, which previously had been very animated, was hushed and deserted, but we were being observed from behind the huts by a few of the villagers, who kept their distance. We reclothed the figure and returned it to its ritual place. . . . Nine days later . . . we were not surprised to learn that cases of smallpox had broken out in the village, but the villagers considered that we had caused it. . . .'[146] Fortunately for Hottot and his companions the villagers thought that they must have very great spiritual power, not to have been harmed themselves for interfering with the fetish. Hottot's offence seems to have been both in moving the figure out of the hut which was its proper place and in removing the clothing.

Some sculptures are kept wrapped up and hidden from sight except when the rituals are performed. The Yoruba figures which commemorate deceased twins are commonly wrapped up in cloths and kept in a calabash by their mother, while in Ife ancient terracotta sculptures are reported sometimes to be buried in the ground between festivals.

161 Terracotta head of a ram used in the cult of Orisha Iko at the Omitoto Grove in Ife. Chief Obaloran who is in charge of the cult is not allowed to see it. For safety, however, he has placed it, on loan, in the Ife Museum. L. 6 in.

162 Bronze figure of Onile, the
owner of the earth, the spirit whose
cult, the Ogboni Society, was one of
the main political forces among the
Yoruba. This figure, thought to have
been made in the eighteenth century,
was formerly used in the Ogboni
house at Apomu. Nigerian Museum,
Lagos. Ht 29¼ in.

163 Face-mask for the *egungun* cult which is primarily concerned with funeral ceremonies, but also provides entertainment. The wearer looks out through the eyes. Collected by Frobenius in Northern Yorubaland in 1912. Museum für Völkerkunde, Berlin. Ht 11 in.

Even when in use, some sculptures may only be looked upon by certain members of the society. Horton reports the case of the shrine of the head of the village heroes of Soku, where even the priest does not see the cult object, which is hidden behind a screen of skulls of sacrificed animals.[147] Very commonly, membership of masked societies is restricted to one sex. Around the Plateau of northern Nigeria there are several small groups of people whose womenfolk are forbidden to see the masks used by the men, and take great joy, therefore, in visiting the museum at Jos where the masks are openly displayed.

Of course, most people interested in African sculpture are unable to see it in use, and must form their own impressions from museum displays. A museum usually possesses only the wooden part of a mask, which it may display under a spotlight which projects a single interpretation of the sculpture. Kenneth Murray has pointed out that masks 'are intended to be seen in movement in a dance; frequently one which is inferior when held in the hand looks more effective than a finer carving when seen with its costume. It is, moreover, essential to see masks in use before judging what they express, for it is easy to read into an isolated mask what was never meant to be there.'[148] Chinua Achebe in his novel *The Arrow of God*[149] brings this out very well. One of his characters, Edogo, is a carver. 'When he had finished carving the face and head he had been a little disappointed. . . . But the owners of the work had not complained; in fact they had praised it very highly. Edogo knew, however, that he must see the

Mask in action to know whether it was good or bad.' To appreciate the carving as it was conceived by the artist, we need to see it in movement, possibly above eye-level, and perhaps illuminated by the intermittent light of torches. Moreover, to isolate the mask is to take it out of its meaningful context, for the mask itself is regarded merely as a part of a complex – part of a costume which is danced in to music – and it is only when all these elements are present that the mask comes to life, becomes inhabited by the spirit. One would like to see the entire complex recorded in the field by ciné camera with synchronized sound; then perhaps in the museum the masks and costumes could be mounted on animated figures like those which have made Disneyland famous, to perform the dances to the original music. But even this would convey only a small part of the original, for the atmosphere of excitement, mingled with awe and even fear, would still be missing.

The emphasis which museums inevitably place on the mask may often mislead us in another way, for the mask may be the least significant element in the complex. Among the Yoruba, the *egungun*

164 Headpiece for the *egungun* cult carved by Adugbologe of Abeokuta. The four attached figures may be by his son Ayo. British Museum W. 15⅛ in

Ill. 163

Ills. 164, 166

Ill. 165 dancers of the ancestor cult in some areas wear masks which cover the face, in others head-pieces, and elsewhere costumes without any sculptures at all. Among the Kissi in Guinea, initiates wear fibre costumes, but paint their faces instead of wearing masks,[150] and Ngere girls after initiation paint their faces in brilliant colours and their upper torsos white.[151]

Not only are many figure sculptures not normally seen but many African masks are not seen at all even when they are in use! Robin Horton, in describing the sculpture of the Kalabari, has shown that many of their masks such as the *otobo* masks, which represent a water spirit with human and hippopotamus features, are worn on top of the dancer's head, so that the main features of the sculpture are facing the sky, while the mask as a whole is hidden from spectators by a

165 On occasions where masks are worn in some communities, others paint the body, like this Ngere girl prepared for a festival.

166 Members of the *Elewe* group of *egungun* dancers from Ila in Northern Yorubaland. They wear no masks but their faces are hidden by their costumes which are
designed to permit free movement in their athletic dances. Bells above their leather
gaiters sound in rhythm with their movements which are emphasized by the brightly
coloured woollen tassels hanging from the waist.

167 The Kalabari make memorial screens (*duen fobara*) for their most prominent ancestors. They are kept in a conspicuous position in the assembly hall of the house where they used to live. The ship shows that this man was a prominent trader; the heads indicate that he owned many slaves. The rectangular shape and grouping of the figures seems to be derived from Benin plaques, while the construction from separate pieces of wood is probably derived from contact with ships' carpenters. British Museum. Ht 45½ in.

ruff.[152] Probably the best-known and most often exhibited mask of this type is shown in *Ill. 168*: one wonders how many of the people who have admired its sculptural quality realized that it was not made for human gaze. The whole masquerade is directed towards the spirit, not towards the spectator – an excellent example of Margaret Trowell's class of 'spirit-regarding art'.

Horton's study has exploded a number of other generalizations about African art. Because we look upon sculptures as objects of beauty, we imagine that their makers and users do, yet the Kalabari view their sculptures with apathy; even when the spirit is being invoked, the mask is hardly looked at.[153] Indeed, the sculpture may evoke revulsion: a man's ugliness will be compared to a spirit sculpture, or to 'the sculpture of a god by one who does not know how to carve'. Moreover, pregnant women are advised not to look at sculptures 'lest their children acquire its big eyes and long nose, and so turn out ugly'.[154] So little interest is taken by the Kalabari in the appearance of their sculptures that they often keep sculptures of spirits in dark shrines which people may not enter and cannot see into. As we have mentioned, in one case even the priest does not see the sculpture.

In contrast, however, their ancestor memorial screens are intended *Ill. 167* to be seen. Moreover, these constitute another exception to the

168 *Otobo* mask used by the *Ekine* Society among the Kalabari Ijo, to represent a water spirit with human and hippopotamus features. This fine sculpture has been much admired in exhibitions, but in use among the Kalabari it was hidden from view by a ruff. Coll. Raymond Wielgus. L. $18\frac{1}{2}$ in.

169, 170 Figures in the Benin style representing Portuguese soldiers show a greater freedom of pose than do the traditional representations of court officials like that of the messenger. This may be due to Portuguese influence. Sixteenth or seventeenth century. Nigerian Museum, Lagos. Hts $17\frac{1}{4}$, 25 in.

generally accepted idea that African sculpture is monoxylous, i.e. carved out of a single block of wood, for they are constructed from separately carved sections which have been fitted together. This carpentry may reflect European influence resulting from the palm-oil trade in the Niger Delta, for these screens seem to have been constructed only since the eighteenth century, perhaps modelled in form on the rectangular bronze plaques at Benin, which in turn seem to have been ultimately inspired by European woodcuts in books.

Ills. 171, 251

Not all Kalabari masks are hidden from view, of course. The central character of the Ngbula play, for example, is a native doctor whose ugliness, which is emphasized in the head-piece, helps him to drive away evil spirits.[155] Horton points out that the Kalabari do not possess any masks which represent beauty, in contrast to some Ibo groups who have pairs of masks representing ugliness (the elephant spirit) and beauty (the maiden spirit).

Ills. 172, 173

It has been found too that masks of similar appearance may be used in different ways. Vandenhoute has shown that although the masks used along the Upper Cavally River in the Ivory Coast by the Dan, Ngere (or Gere or Kran) and Wobe vary in their ranking and function, this differentiation is not related to their appearance. For them the mask is a channel of communication with the high god Zlan, but the real intermediaries are the spirits of the ancestors who are invoked through the mask. The power of the mask to influence the ancestors depends on the social prestige of the owner, since a man can only reach prominence with their help, and his very success shows that the ancestors favour him. An inherited mask retains its power over the ancestors and the more prestigious its owner was in this life, the more powerful he will be as an ancestor. Similarly, old masks which span several generations are considered especially powerful. The prestige of a mask is thus an acquired characteristic which cannot be deduced from its appearance, but only from the appropriate information acquired in the field.

Again, Dan masks of identical appearance may have quite different functions and these too are classified into categories of higher and lower rank. The use of the masks is regulated by the *go*-master, the priest of *go*, the highest imaginable power. In his hut there is not only the potent fetish which is the source of his power but also the actual presence of the ancestors, for it is in his hut that prominent people are buried and their masks preserved. These masks are of the

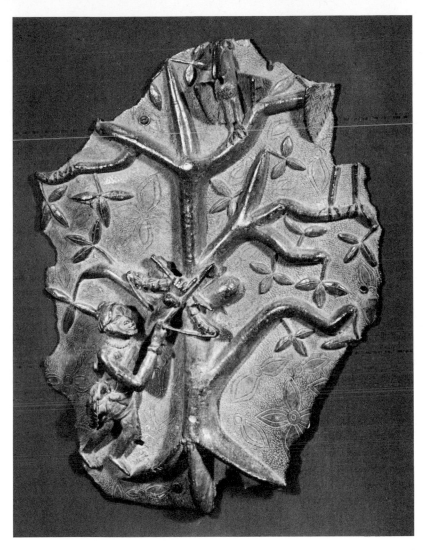

171 Broken bronze plaque from the Palace in Benin. The unusual arrangement of
the huntsman in what appears to be an attempt at perspective, together with the
rectangular shape of the unbroken plaques, suggest that the artist may have seen
European book illustrations. William Fagg has called the artist 'The Master of the
Leopard Hunt'. His work is much less rigid and more imaginative than the majority
of the plaques, like *Ill. 251*, and this might indicate that he was the first to make this
type of casting. Certainly Benin traditions indicate that the idea of making these
plaques was suggested by a Portuguese. Probably sixteenth century. Museum für
Völkerkunde, Berlin. Ht 18 in.

172 Maiden spirit mask, *Mmwo Ogbegu*, symbolizing beauty, used in an *Ekpe* play at Awkusu, Onitsha Ibo. Nigerian Museum, Lagos. Ht 8⅜ in.

173 Mask representing the Elephant Spirit, symbol of ugliness, used by the *Ekpe* Society of the Aba Asa Clan, Owerri Ibo. The ears, tusks and horns have been carved separately and attached. Nigerian Museum, Lagos. Ht 19 in.

highest rank, followed by sacrificial masks upon which heads of families sacrifice to their ancestors. Then come avenging masks, who act as police and judiciary combined; these sometimes act independently of the *go*-master, thus forcing him to employ one of his highest-ranking masks in order to maintain his authority. Other high-ranking masks include those used at initiation, not only to teach the initiates, but also to entertain those who have remained behind in the village. Communities on the edges of the forest and savanna have the *sagbwe* masks, with their own hierarchy; their task is to protect the village, especially from fire, which is a major hazard. The lower categories are described as dancing, singing, begging and palaver masks, and are mainly intended to entertain, though they often teach as well. Even when these perform, fear of the supernatural can sometimes be detected in their audiences. Now masks can move up these hierarchies – usually on the death of their owner, if he has achieved eminence in his lifetime. Thus there is no correlation between rank or function and the form of a mask.

Masks may also be demoted if they prove ineffective or get damaged, for they have to be beautiful in order to please the ancestors. Formerly, damaged masks were thrown away, but nowadays they are often sold to Europeans. This is one reason why many of the examples in museums are inadequately documented.[156]

Himmelheber, however, denies that the Dan masks are used in the ancestor cult; he maintains that they are the materialization of spirits which live in the bush and which reveal themselves to individuals because they wish to take part in the life of human beings. The masks have three types of head-dress corresponding to three major groups of mask. A tall conical head-dress indicating 'beautiful' is

Ills. 174, 175 worn with the *Dea* mask which is concerned with the circumcision of the youths. There are two types of *Dea* mask, one of which is responsible for teaching the initiates and for frightening away women and children from the initiation camp, and the other for collecting food from the mothers of the youths. These masks are carved to look like a beautiful woman, to make the mask likeable and to keep the initiates happy. A huge feather crown which indicates that a mask is frightening or imposing is worn by several types of mask, all of which have social responsibilities – whether peace-makers (large masks with animal-like features and a moveable lower jaw), or *Gor* society masks, or in the northern savanna area, running masks

184

174, 175 *Dea* mask of the Dan of Ivory Coast and Liberia. The interior shows the marks left by the adze, but it is free from jagged edges which would make it uncomfortable to wear. Masks of this and of several other types are used by the *Poro* Society, though this does not seem to have been their original purpose. Coll. F. Willett. Ht 9½ in.

concerned with fire-fighting. This last group is clearly the *sagbwe* group mentioned by Vandenhoute. The first two appear to correspond to his category of avenging masks, for the *Gor* society mask is very similar in function to the peace-making mask, with which it has joined forces in many places. If there is no peace-making mask in a town, a mask of lower rank may be promoted to act for the *Gor* society: in this respect Himmelheber confirms Vandenhoute's assertion that the form may not be an index of the function of a mask. Himmelheber's third group of masks are those intended purely for entertainment, which wear a sort of wig made from cotton cloth. These are of two kinds, dancing masks which can be of any form,

176, 177, 178 Each medium may have its own style. Azande wood sculptures are much more stylized than their pottery sculpture. The two figures are thought to represent ancestors and to have been used in the rituals of the *Mani* Society. British Museum. Hts $31\frac{1}{2}$, $20\frac{3}{4}$ and 13 in.

179, 180, 181 The Mangbetu, who are neighbours of the Azande use a similar style in both
pottery and wood sculpture. The deformation of
the head reflects their own practice of binding
their babies' heads to make them long and beautiful. The effect is heightened by a tall and often
expanding hair-style which is also represented in
the sculpture. British Museum. Hts 10, 7 and 28 in.

though the most frequent type has a human face with short tubular eyes and duiker horns carved across the top, and fault-finding masks, which play very roughly, whipping bystanders whom they have tricked into misbehaving, e.g. by laughing at a mask which represents a deformity.[157]

Girard, working among the Wobe, has given us yet a different picture.[158] He tells us that a group of pure spirits, *kosri*, gave the laws of social organization to the first men and these separated them from the animals. Each law was symbolized by a great mask made to resemble the spirit which gave it. Girard insists that the mask among the Wobe, Ngere and Yacuba (who appear to be a sub-group of the Dan) never represents a woman's face, but is instead a symbol of virility, for the mask lies at the origin of the differentiation of the sexes. At first the sexes were indistinguishable. When one group acquired the first mask from the *kosri*, its members also acquired virility at the same time, together with superiority over the other group, which developed feminine characters. At the same time, the first men received from the *kosri* the secret societies which were already in two groups. One group drew its power from that of the ancestors, forming societies of the great masks, while the other group derived its power from the *kosri*. Thus, from the beginning, spirits and ancestors have been involved in the masks, but whatever their source of power, the great masks function in the same way. Later still the spirit of the ancestors, *Gnon Soa*, had to give the lesser masks, made in his own likeness, to later men. In general Girard's account is a refinement, not a complete contradiction of Vandenhoute's. Indeed, he shows that although there is a fixed hierarchy of masks, in any one village the principal mask, and therefore the most powerful one, may be chosen from any of the masks the village possesses. Although the picture of the role of the mask in these related groups is confusing, all three accounts make it clear that the appearance of a mask is not an absolutely reliable guide to its rank or function.

STYLE IN AFRICAN SCULPTURE

Examples of African sculpture exhibited in museums or illustrated in books on African art are commonly considered to be representative of the style of the people from whom they were collected. William Fagg, for example, writes that 'every tribe is, from the point of view of art, a universe to itself. . . . The tribe . . . uses art among many other

182 White-faced mask of a type used by the BaKota, BaLumbo, BaPunu, Mpongwe and several other tribes. Documented pieces have been collected among all these peoples. Among the BaPunu the wearer dances on stilts. Rietberg Museum, Zürich. Ht $11\frac{3}{4}$ in.

183 Wooden figures covered with brass or copper sheeting are placed by the BaKota over a package containing sample bones of outstanding ancestors. Siroto suggests that the form was developed to display as much of the valuable metal as possible. Certainly its two-dimensional character attracted Western painters; Juan Gris made a copy of one in cardboard in 1922. British Museum. Ht 26 in.

means to express its internal solidarity and self-sufficiency, and conversely its difference from all others.'[159] He goes on to mention several instances where adjacent peoples share stylistic features, but his plates, chosen one from each 'artistic universe', do not adequately indicate the complexity of the situation. Only where the range of art objects is very limited can a single work be considered fully typical of a style, but there are many societies where different art styles are used in different contexts, for example when a mask-using cult has been introduced from an adjacent area, as has happened in the case of

Ill. 183
Ill. 182

the BaKota, whose reliquary figures are highly distinctive, but whose white-faced masks cannot be distinguished stylistically from those of the BaLumbo or BaPunu, from whose area of the Ogowe River the cult seems to be derived. The BaBembe from the eastern Congo have a variety of markedly different art styles, each associated with a different cult group, none of which is found throughout Bembeland, so that one cannot speak of a BaBembe style.[160] Olbrechts pointed out in 1946 that in the Congo masks are usually employed by societies whose ramifications extend through territories much larger than those of regional styles, so that the mask style is commonly quite

184 The figures of the Bena Lulua are highly distinctive. They show elaborate scarifications and usually have the navel emphasized. British Museum. Ht $19\frac{5}{16}$ in.

185 The BaKuba have a great variety of masks, many of which have been taken over by their neighbours. This, the *mwaash a mboy* type, is worn at the initiation rites to symbolize the culture hero Woot who originated royalty, the political structure and most of the arts and crafts. The superstructure of the mask appears to represent the trunk of an elephant (on some examples it has tusks) which is a royal emblem. The mask may only be worn by men of royal descent. (Collected about 1892 by the Afro–American missionary W.H. Sheppard.) Hampton Institute, Hampton, Virginia. Ht $16\frac{1}{8}$ in.

186 The Dan and Ngere modes of sculpture contrast strongly yet the same sculptors carve in both styles. Contrast the cubistic construction of this face in the Ngere mode with that of *Ill. 174*. Liberia. Yale University Art Gallery. Gift of Mr & Mrs James Osborn for the Linton Collection of African Art. Ht 9 in.

Ills. 184, 185
Ill. 189

alien to that of the statuary; for example, masks of the Bena Lulua are quite unlike their figures, but very similar to the masks of the neighbouring BaKuba; while BaPende masks too are widespread among their neighbours.[161] Yet a widespread cult group, instead of distributing a single mask type throughout its area of influence, may use a variety of different styles. The *Poro* Society is found in Sierra Leone, Guinea, Liberia and the Ivory Coast; it employs the sleek moderately naturalistic masks associated with the name 'Dan'

Ills. 174, 186
and the violently contrasting Ngere masks, which are highly cubistic

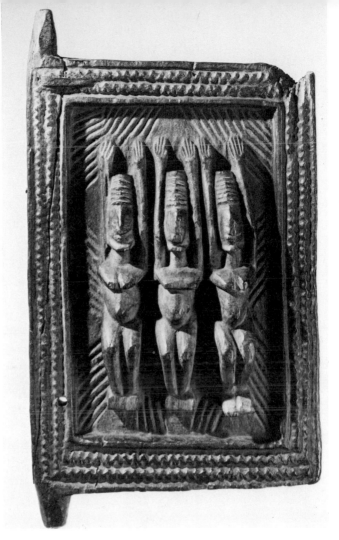

187 Door for a granary decorated with figures of ancestors in a very simplified style. Dogon. Musée de l'Homme, Paris. Ht 15½ in.

in style and often only roughly finished. Moreover, Vandenhoute has shown that these contrasting styles may both be carved by the same individual artist.[162] Without apparent external influence the Dogon have developed three distinctive styles, the very simplified forms used on their masks, the solid cubistic figures of ancestors used *Ill. 111* as decorative motifs, e.g. on doors, and the spindly, knobbly style of *Ill. 187* their free-standing ancestor figures, though the latter two sometimes occur in the same piece; when for example the main figure carved in the third style may sit on a stool with legs carved in the second. *Ill. 190*

193

Again Olbrechts pointed out that stylistic elements can be borrowed; BaYaka eyes and the elbows-on-knees pose of BaPende caryatid figures both appear to be derived from the BaJokwe.[163]

One aspect of the phenomenon seems so far to have been over-looked – that masks may be diffused independently of the cult in which they are traditionally used. In Ishan, north-east of Benin, in

Ill. 191

1959, I found that the masks used in the boys' masquerade dances had all been carved by Ibibio carvers in Ikot Ekpene, well over a hundred and fifty miles away across the other side of the River Niger, yet in one village I was told that they were carved by a local carver who happened to be away during my visit. My companion, Dr R.E. Bradbury at the same time bought a figure carved in the traditional

188, 189 The BaPende have an even greater variety of masks than the BaKuba. This type, *mbuya*, is used in the ceremonies which follow initiation, to represent an important person in BaPende society. Although they represent roles in the secular society rather than spirits they are used also to control supernatural forces. The person who has benefited from their intervention may be required to wear a miniature copy of the mask, usually in ivory, as a pendant. British Museum. Ht *c.* $2\frac{1}{2}$ in. Private Collection: Ht $12\frac{1}{2}$ in.

190 Figure of a Dogon ancestor in a spindly style, sitting on a stool whose legs represent ancestors carved in the style of those on the door (*Ill. 187*). University Museum, Philadelphia, Pennsylvania. Ht 25 in.

191 Mask carved by an Ibibio in Ikot Ekpene but used in a masquerade by uninitiated boys in Ishan, a hundred and fifty miles away. Coll. F. Willett. Ht 11⅛ in.

Ishan style. The people who sold us these pieces did not seem to distinguish between the indigenous and the imported style. In another Ishan village I bought a typical Ikot Ekpene doll from an old lady who declared that she had had it since she was a child, which suggests that the trade in Ibibio sculptures is not a very recent phenomenon.

Ill. 194

Even more remarkable is John Picton's observation: 'on Igbira masquerades I have seen the following types of masks: native Igbira carving, masks in the style of the northern Edo peoples, Yoruba *gelede* masks from near Lagos, Ibibio masks from Ikot Ekpene (these latter two types presumably traded by diverse routes), an ebony face carved for Europeans, and a mask carved by Basa Nge. That is six different art styles fulfilling for Igbira the same ritual function.'[164]

Ills. 65, 191

Ill. 205

192 Masks are often carved in a style completely different from that used for figure sculpture. This mask used by the BaTeke is in striking contrast to their figure sculpture (*Ills. 150–152*). Formerly owned by André Derain. Ht 13$\frac{3}{8}$ in.

193 *Left:* Wooden figure of the BaYanzi, called *mpuwu* and said to protect the village. *Right:* Wooden figure from the roof of the hut of the chief's senior wife, in which the regalia are kept. BaPende. Musée Royal de l'Afrique Centrale, Tervuren. Hts 39$\frac{3}{8}$, 43$\frac{7}{8}$ in.

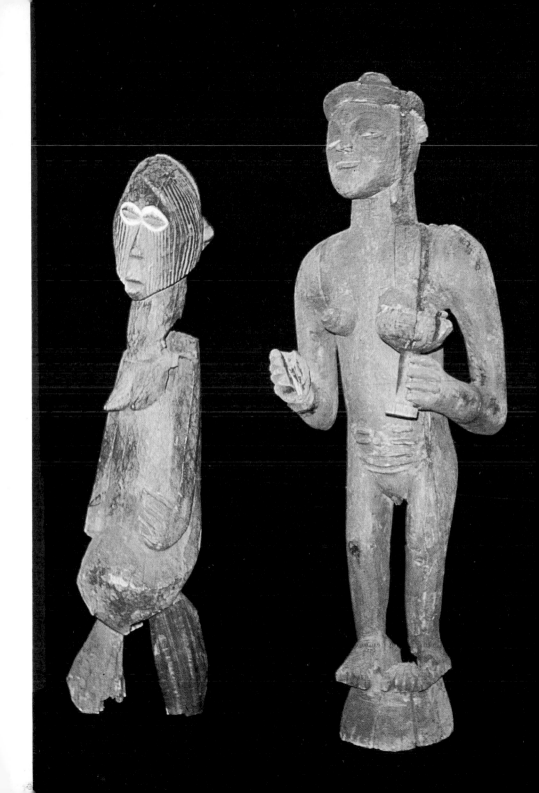

William Fagg himself acknowledges that it is possible for one tribal style to influence another, but he regards this as exceptional. Yet he considers the basic philosophy of all African, as indeed of all tribally organized societies, as being one, a desire to promote increase of the life force in their own kind, their crops, their stock and the animals they hunt, a notion which he sees expressed in the art by exponential curves, curves of constantly increasing radius which are found in all growing organisms, being especially clearly seen in animal horns and in the shells of snails. Fagg detects these curves in sculptures from all over Africa (and from all other tribally organized societies such as the Old Stone Age artists of Europe), which seems to be somewhat inconsistent with his idea of 'tribality', of the hermetically sealed tribal universe. While it is probably true that African religions are all concerned with fertility and increase, it does not necessarily follow that every horn represented in a sculpture is a symbol of fertility. Sacrifices are an integral part of all African religions and usually some form of food is offered. Horned animals are the most valuable creatures to be sacrificed and their skulls are commonly kept on the altar as a tally, a reminder to the god or

194 The use of Ibibio sculptures in Ishan is not recent, for this Ikot Ekpene doll was bought there from an old lady who declared that she had had it since her childhood. Coll. F. Willett. Ht $12\frac{1}{4}$ in.

195, 196 Two old Ibibio masks representing spirits, made for the *Ekpo* Society to which all adult males used to belong. Its duties involved propitiation of the spirits of the ancestors and the maintenance of the social order by supporting the elders. British Museum. Hts 9½, 15¼ in.

197 Some African peoples have been strongly influenced by the art styles of their neighbours. These Idoma sculptures reflect influence from the Ibo to their south. *Left:* Dance headpiece for the *Ogrinya* Society of men who had killed an elephant, a lion or a man. British Museum. Ht 10 in. *Right:* Figure for the spirit *Anjenu,* used to effect cures or bring good luck. Coll. W.B. Fagg. Ht 15 in.

198, 199 A group of Ishan men who now live and work in Ibadan still perform the traditional acrobatic dance *Ikhien-ani-mhin* of their home area. The acrobats wear bright costumes with a net covering the face but they are accompanied by a figure who wears an Ibibio mask from Ikot Ekpene, similar to *Ill. 191*.

200 An ancestor altar in Chief Oghiamien's house in Benin. The heads are of wood plated with brass sheet. The tall objects are rattles used to invoke the spirits. Blood from sacrificial animals can be seen on the altar while the skulls of sacrificed animals hang above as a tally.

201 (*left*) Fetish figure of the BaSongye. The horn on the head contains magical substances. Unfortunately, little is known about the precise purpose of these striking sculptures. Musée Royal de l'Afrique Centrale, Tervuren. Ht 34⅜ in.

202 (*above*) 'Hunting' fetish from the BaKuba. Although the sculpture is in BaKuba style, the horn on the head appears to be derived from the BaSongye. British Museum. Ht 18¼ in.

ancestor of the sacrifices that have been made and at the same time a *Ill. 200* display of the devotion of his worshippers. Sometimes these horns and the shells of edible snails are attached to the statues. Being hollow, they provide natural containers and are commonly used to contain magical substances, i.e. fetish material. Vandenhoute says that 'for- *Ills. 201, 202* merly ram's horns filled with magical substances used to be attached to the hair-dressing of notable warriors, originally as a protective amulet in time of war then as a mark of honour. The forehead tresses of the popular hair-style are copied from this decoration with ram's horns.' These horns are now represented carved on the mask. Similarly, he reports that masks sometimes still have horns filled with magical substances attached to them.[165] John Boston tells us that among the northern Ibo in some cases real horns are attached to the mask while in others they are represented by the sculptor. 'The custom of using horns in this way can be related to the communal hunts

for wild animals which were traditionally carried out by young men, in order to win renown for their age-groups. Today these quests have been transferred to other fields, such as feast-giving and road and house building, and the head-dress is no longer an actual trophy. But it conveys the same symbolism of masculinity, and is still used in performances to draw an analogy between the physical perfection of
Ill. 204 wild animals and the strength and vitality of young men.'[166] Exponential curves are found too in the canine teeth of carnivores and the talons of birds of prey which are, like the horns of small antelopes, commonly used as personal ornaments, e.g. in necklaces and head-dresses. The symbolism here would appear to suggest that the wearer seeks to share in the courage, strength, or swiftness of these creatures (unless indeed they are purely ornamental). Horns and shells, then, appear in contexts which do not seem to be directly concerned with increase and fertility and it therefore seems unlikely that every exponential curve in a sculpture is a sign of increase. Indeed, many of the so-called 'horns' on the heads of human figures have been regarded by other workers as hair-styles, e.g. in the drinking-cups of the
Ill. 203 BaKuba. Of course, it could be argued that the hair is dressed in this way to imitate animal horns and thus the symbolism is merely less directly expressed. However, no field-worker has yet produced evidence that exponential curves are either conscious or unconscious expressions by African artists of a desire for increase. Until this is documented unequivocally in the field, from outside the area of Bantu-speaking Africa (where at least the philosophical basis has been demonstrated by Father Placide Tempels) it is best to keep an open mind on this issue. In fairness to the author of this theory it should be pointed out that he himself regards it as a tentative hypothesis which may never be proved: it is some of his followers who have elevated it to a doctrine.

While it is probably an exaggeration to regard each African art style as incomprehensible to neighbouring peoples, an investigation by John Picton among the Igbira throws an interesting light on the problem. An old carver, Amodu Ihiovi, examined a fine Basa Nge
Ill. 205 mask with elongated, almost reptilian features, which Picton had just obtained for the Nigerian Museum. 'He chuckled with delight, admiring it for some time and saying that the man who carved it knew how to carve. But then he said it would have been better if the mouth had been placed higher up the face, and if the nose had only

203 Wooden cup for a chief. The elaborate horns may represent a hairdressing. BaMbala, a subdivision of the BaKuba. British Museum. Ht 8 in.

204 Northern Ibo mask with large carved horns, reminding viewers of the communal hunts conducted by young men for the enhancement of the reputation of their age-group. Nigerian Museum, Lagos. Ht 24 in.

205 Mask collected in the Eganyi district of Igbira (about midway between Okene and the River Niger) carved in the early years of this century by a Basa Nge sculptor. This is the mask on which the Igbira carver Ihiovi commented. Nigerian Museum, Lagos. L. 22 in.

been about half as long, and if the top of the head had not been as tall. Of course, if all this were so it would look just like a typical Igbira mask!'[167] Evidently this carver knew what he liked, and liked what he knew so that it appears that one carver is highly resistant to change in a society which is quite eclectic in its choice of masks.

AESTHETICS IN AFRICAN SCULPTURE

How does this affect our understanding of African art? Are there absolute standards of beauty which operate transculturally as the large variety of masks used among the Igbira appears to imply, or is there a specific aesthetic for each society, as the judgment of the Igbira carver Amodu Ihiovi would suggest? It is obvious in our own society that artistic appreciation is not on the same level throughout the community: artists and art critics cultivate their awareness of artistic values in a way not shared by large sections of the community. If we wish to gain an understanding of contemporary art we would probably have to obtain our information mainly from art critics, secondarily from the relatively few artists who are articulate in the

206 Wooden stool for a queen mother, decorated with silver sheeting, Ashanti. Stools in forms related to this are found among the other Akan peoples (e.g. the Anyi and the Baule), among the Fon in Dahomey and the Duala in Cameroun. British Museum. Ht 16 in.

207 Mask carved in the early years of this century by Ihiovi of Opopocho village, Ihima district of Igbira. The objects on top of the mask include magical 'medicines' and the remains of sacrifices, for the mask is still in use.

verbal expression of their ideas and, while we might talk to people at exhibitions of art, we would probably not interview people at random in the streets. The same problem exists in studying African art but in this case the critics might be difficult to identify.

A great deal more work needs to be done on this aspect of African art, but several interesting studies have already been carried out in different ways with different groups. Some have concentrated on the artist, his incentives and training, showing how works of art come to be created, while others have concentrated on the art objects themselves and the judgments passed on them; in one case we have a comparative evaluation of sculpture by Africans and by Americans.

Whatever the approach, it is clearly necessary to take as our starting-point the society in which the art objects were made. Hans Himmelheber was the first to attempt to investigate the standards of beauty applied in Africa. His study of the artists of the Guro and Atutu published in 1935 showed that there clearly are standards of beauty, for he found that a client might refuse to accept a mask if it were not beautiful enough, or the payment made to the sculptor might depend on the beauty of the sculpture. He conducted a series of simple experiments by getting his porters to point out the pieces they preferred from among those he had collected; he invited artists and other people to do the same. This was done repeatedly, and always the same three pieces were picked out as the best, and they were the three which he preferred himself. When he attempted to get them to explain their preferences he got only rather vague replies, but he appears to have been asking them, through interpreters, about their 'beauty of line' and 'power of expression', so it is little wonder that he came up against 'a wall of incomprehension'.[168]

More successful, however, was his discovery that both masks and figures were intended to be likenesses of their living subject. In many cases his informants were able to name the person represented without any hesitation, recognizing him by the features of the sculpture, not by his scarification pattern. To non-Africans the faces of these sculptures seem undifferentiated and expressionless, but both the Guro and the Atutu said that feeling was shown by the mouth of the carving. Indeed the mouth is the liveliest part of an African face.

Others have followed Himmelheber in these studies, attempting to establish the criteria by which sculpture is judged in the society of its origin. Vandenhoute conducted a number of experiments among the Dan of the Ivory Coast. Pieces he used have been illustrated by Gerbrands.[169] Of three masks which he had carved himself, a Lome[170] sculptor called Yituwo chose as best one which had a fringe of stylized horns over the forehead, a feature of which he was particularly proud. When three more masks were added he, as well as the local chief and various old men, agreed in selecting a different mask because it was more carefully finished and a better colour, despite the fact that the eye was slightly damaged, the tip of the nose worn, and the lines above the eyes not quite straight. In another experiment, the sculptor Uwi Magbwe, a Gulome,[171] preferred, out of a group of his own masks, one with a hair-dressing carved in a way which he had originated. The choice was confirmed by old men of the village. As a result of such experiments Vandenhoute was able to formulate as the Dan criteria of beauty symmetry about the vertical axis, coupled with balance, rhythm and harmony between the various masses, surfaces and lines, criteria which we tend to appreciate intuitively, rather than measure in an objective way. Vandenhoute pointed out that his informants did not indicate these criteria in words, but that the carver demonstrates his appreciation of them by continually pausing to assess his work, sometimes holding it upside-down or back to front, screwing up his eyes and holding the mask at arm's length. This is the thinking which the artist declared to be the hardest part of the work, as other Dan artists in north-eastern Liberia did later to Fischer, for this is the crucial stage in achieving in wood the image conceived in the artist's mind. In the European tradition, the artist can experiment beforehand in his sketch-book and copy from this the elements of his final work; the African artist has to visualize his finished work from the beginning and carry it in his mind continuously. Additional criteria Vandenhoute found were those of finish (both polish and the colour) and of use, i.e. comfort in wear so that the wearer can see and breathe well.[172] *Ills. 174* and *175* show how well these masks are finished inside as well as out.

Among other Dan groups in north-eastern Liberia, Fischer's informants, unlike Vandenhoute's, told him that a sculptor will often carve spontaneously, inspired by a beautiful face, but without attempting simply to represent what they have seen. Indeed, a spoon carved by Tompieme using his daughter as a model was criticized by another carver, Si: 'That isn't carved, it's a photograph.' Fischer interprets this as meaning that Tompieme has not succeeded in

Ill. 208

208 Head of a spoon carved by Tompieme, and his daughter whom it portrays.

transposing and abstracting the carving to the degree necessary for it to become a work of art.[173]

Such observations have rarely been recorded. It seems usually to have been assumed that there was no vocabulary in African languages to permit aesthetics to be studied. Robert Thompson, however, solicited from about two hundred Yoruba informants criticisms of a number of sculptures.[174] He recorded their comments fully in Yoruba and then analysed the frequency with which reference was made to various criteria. Nineteen criteria were mentioned, the most frequent being *jijora*, the moderate resemblance to the subject, a balance between the extremes of portraiture and abstraction. He was told repeatedly of a pair of twin figures that 'they look like somebody'. It is indeed one of the surprises of living in Yorubaland that one does frequently see people whose features remind one very

209, 210 Although African sculpture often strikes the viewer as highly stylized, surprising resemblances to real people can sometimes be observed. This Yoruba twin figure carved in Ila is remarkably similar to Miss Yemi Idowu, who represented Nigeria in the 1963 'Miss United Nations' contest. Coll. Michelle Treiman. Ht $11\frac{1}{4}$ in.

forcibly of a particular sculptural style, yet the sculptures are not portraits of individuals, but they are supposed to look as if they might be. A second quality is *ifarahon*, visibility; the various parts of a sculpture should be clearly formed both in the initial stage of blocking out of the masses and in the later stages of finishing the details with a knife. Equally important is *didon*, luminosity, or shining smoothness of surface, so that the whole sculpture offers a play of light and shade. Another criterion is *gigun*, a straight upright posture and symmetrical arrangement of the parts of the sculpture. This does not exclude asymmetry, but it does restrict it to fairly minor details. *Odo* is also important, the representation of the subject in the prime of life. A sculpture is also expected to show 'coolness' or composure, *tutu*, a quality which is sought in human behaviour too. In sculpture it is shown by the absence of violence in the facial expression or gesture;

211 Staff carried by a devotee, from the Temple of Shongo, the thunder god, in Ogbomosho. This sculpture shows the aesthetic qualities which characterize Yoruba sculpture. Coll. Anne d'Harnoncourt. Ht 16½ in.

212 BaLega figure in ivory, collected by Daniel Biebuyck in 1952. It was owned by a member of the highest level of the *kindi* grade of the *Bwami* society. It is called 'One-Arm' and represents the physical and moral harm that results from undue interference in other people's affairs. Coll. Daniel Biebuyck. Ht 5¼ in.

in the dance by the withdrawn expressionless face of the dancer; the chief should always behave calmly and unemotionally. This last criterion has been reported also by Warren D'Azevedo among the Gola of Liberia: 'The pinnacle of success . . . comes with the ability to be nonchalant at the right moment . . . to reveal no emotion in situations where excitement and sentimentality are acceptable – in other words to act as though one's mind were in another world. It is particularly admirable to do difficult tasks with an air of ease and silent disdain. Women are admired for a surly detached expression, and somnambulistic movement and attitude during the dance or other performance is considered very attractive.'[175]

Some of the criteria which Thompson was able to elicit by general discussions, rather than by direct questioning, which can produce misleading answers, have sometimes been remarked upon by sensitive Western observers of Yoruba sculpture – the moderate naturalism has always been pointed out; the careful finish has been observed but not always mentioned; the symmetry of pose is generally regarded as a basic African characteristic, as is the portrayal of human beings in their prime; balanced visibility and composure of expression seem not to have been expressly remarked, yet they are obviously there to be seen in all good Yoruba sculpture. The judgment of sympathetic non-African observers such as experienced curators of collections of African art would probably agree with the Yoruba about which Yoruba sculptures are good and which bad, even without knowing the criteria Thompson has determined; yet without the demonstration of these standards in the field we should not have been justified in inferring them. In more recent field-work, Thompson has been able to show that the concept of 'coolness' is admired in the other arts as well and is a reflection of a moral ideal, while the evidence from the Gola suggests that this ideal may be widespread. Armed with Thompson's list of Yoruba criteria, the Western critic is better able to check his own intuitive judgments of the sculpture by reference to the qualities the artist had to seek. *Ills. 211, 23, 68, 94, 226–32, 242, 243*

The fact that some of these standards had been remarked before Thompson's analysis should not be allowed to mislead us into thinking that Western sensitivity will produce judgments in all works of African art which will coincide with the standards of their makers. Among the BaLega, for example, Biebuyck found that all the traditional sculptures used by the *Bwami* society in their rituals were *Ills. 212, 213* judged to be 'good' by which was meant that they fulfilled their functions. 'Criticism of the physical appearance . . . is inconceivable.'[176] As a result, celluloid dolls obtained by trade enjoy equal regard with the traditional sculptures in ivory and wood. This is surprising because the traditional objects serve to demonstrate membership in the prestigious association – only initiated members may possess them; moreover, each of them is associated with a proverb which expresses the ideal of moral beauty to which initiates aspire. It seems strange that objects which are presumably inexpensive and easily obtained should be accepted for use in the relatively exclusive society. Yet Biebuyck observed that the possession of large numbers of the traditional objects reflected great prestige for the owner, for in order to acquire them he must have taken part in a great many rituals and have served as head of the funerary ceremonies of other high-grade members, since they are acquired chiefly by inheritance. It is this very fact, however, which explains the acceptance of the foreign artefact, for the numbers alone are what matters, the quality and age of the pieces are of no importance.

The general congruence of judgment of Yoruba and Western critics appears to imply that there are certain common aesthetic standards which operate across cultural frontiers, even though some societies like the BaLega appear deliberately to ignore them. Leon Siroto investigated this possibility.[177] In order to ensure that the results were not culture-bound, he chose to obtain opinions on a series of thirty-nine photographs of BaKwele masks from sixteen male BaKwele informants and from thirteen 'advanced art students and others able to make such judgments' in New Haven, Connecticut. To have asked his African informants to judge European works would have introduced a cultural bias, since the BaKwele would have been unfamiliar with art objects in other styles, whereas his American informants were familiar with a wide range of artistic styles, and were thus aesthetically less culture-bound. Siroto points out the disadvantage of using photographs rather than originals, in that his New Haven informants were accustomed to interpreting photographs, whereas his BaKwele informants were not, although they were selected for their experience in making or using masks. Eight of the photographs were found to mislead his BaKwele informants, whose judgments were more consistent when these particular examples were omitted. The informants were asked to choose the four most beautiful

Ill. 215

213 BaLega mask carved in ivory and rubbed regularly with palm oil with the same care that initiates of the *bwami* society anoint themselves. During the initiation ceremonies to the highest grade, *kindi*, such masks may be worn, or merely held in the hand, hung on a fence or laid on the floor. Coll. Pablo Picasso. Ht $7\frac{5}{8}$ in.

masks, then the four most beautiful masks of those which remained. This was repeated till the thirty-nine photographs had been divided up into ten groups, ranked in order of beauty. Scores were given to each photograph in each of these groups from nine to zero, and correlations were calculated between the overall rankings of his New Haven informants taken as a single group, and his BaKwele informants taken not only as a single group but also as groups of four carvers, four cult leaders and eight other informants. In general there was substantial overall agreement between the BaKwele and the New Haven judgments. The agreement between each group of BaKwele informants and the New Haven informants could arise by chance less than once in a hundred times. The agreements between the individual BaKwele carvers, cult leaders and four of the eight other informants with the New Haven judgments could arise by chance less than once in twenty times.

Despite these general agreements, however, there was also clear evidence of disagreement. Two photographs were consistently ranked more highly by all the BaKwele informants than they were by the New Haven group. In contrast the photographs ranked second and third best of the thirty-nine by the consensus of the New Haven informants were not placed in the first four by a single BaKwele. These differences are significant, since the rankings between the BaKwele sub-groups are also consistent with each other, and correlate with each other more highly than any sub-group does with the New Haven consensus. The only inconsistency discovered was in the BaKwele attitude to a group of eight masks which were described as 'fierce' masks. Since these are used to exercise social control, it may be that those who were in a position to exercise power through them looked upon them with favour, whereas those who were dominated by them felt fearful and hence disliked them. It is evident that background knowledge possessed by the BaKwele informants led them to make different judgments from each other as well as from the New Haven critics who judged them entirely by their appearance.

In his investigation of Fang aesthetics Fernandez too found that his informants' background was influential; they were loath to pass judgments on sculptures which had been used on the reliquary boxes containing ancestral bones; something of the religious awe deriving from this use seemed to place them beyond the reach of everyday aesthetic judgment. He found too that artists were unwilling to

214, 215 Representation of the human head with a 'heart-shaped' face formed by two intersecting slices cut from the wood is found across the northern edge of the Congo Basin right into Nigeria. The provenance of masks with this feature is sometimes hard to distinguish. The one on the left was carved by an Ibo at Ngbangba Ikoro, Abiriba, Bende Division, while the other was carved by a BaKwele. 214: Nigerian Museum, Lagos. Ht 8 in. 215: British Museum. Ht $10\frac{1}{2}$ in.

criticize each other's work. Nevertheless he asked eight informants which of twelve figures they liked best and why. The answers referred, of course, to technical qualities – whether the surface was smooth, whether the carving was complete – but they showed an interesting concern with balance (*bibwe*). Legs, arms, shoulders, eyes, breasts, all were expected to be carved to match exactly its opposite member. Without this balance 'the figure would not be a real one – it would have no life or vitality within it'. Fernandez found 'that those features that seemed to have what *we* would call movement or vitality were not those selected by my informants. They generally picked those whose presentation and posture were stolid, formal, even – and perhaps this is the best word – suppressed.'[178] Here then there is a clear opposition of African and Western judgments, for the frontality usually regarded as static by Western writers on African art is precisely what gives the sculpture its vitality for a Fang.

Fernandez found that the sculptor in Fang society is subjected to great pressure from his critics while he is working, and that indeed 'the villagers consider themselves to be the final cause of the statue and apply what social pressures they can to the efficient cause, the carver, to see that the work turns out to their expectations'.[179] The artists thus cannot expect to impose aesthetic acquiescence upon their clients, yet Fernandez never came across a case of a statue being refused. 'The view seemed to prevail that any statue can serve its function atop the reliquary whether it is aesthetically satisfying or not',[180] a view which echoes that of the BaLega, that all *Bwami* figures are good.

Fernandez's study shows clearly the influence of a paper by Paul Bohannan in which he discussed the artist and his critic in Tiv society.[181] Bohannan found that the Tiv were interested in the art but not at all in the artist. The Tiv artists had little to tell him; one said that he liked everything he made equally well; his kinsman, however, without being invited to do so, explained which pieces he liked best and why. Another, engaged in sewing patterns on a cloth with raffia for the resist-dye process in which the oversewn parts would come out undyed, was evidently paying no attention to the design and concentrating on a political discussion. When Bohannan remonstrated he was told 'that one does not look at a pattern until it is finished: then one looks to see if it has come out well. If this one did not come out well, he said, "I will sell it to the Ibo; if it does, I

216, 217 Tiv figure of a woman, with elaborate scarification on the front and back of the trunk. Such figures are set up outside the house of a man's senior wife for the purpose of 'repairing the land'. Cambridge Museum of Archaeology and Ethnology. Ht 18¾ in.

shall keep it. And if it comes out extraordinarily well, I shall give it to my mother-in-law." ' Bohannan found that the bystanders were the critics. A carver was making a figure of a woman when a youngster came up and asked why he had carved three bumps on her belly. The old man told him they were her navel and breasts. The youngster began to object that 'even if they had fallen they would not . . .' whereupon the old man chopped off all three bumps.

Ills. 216, 217

There seemed to be no great sense of the artist's vision, of his creativity, despite the fact that the same word *gba* is used of God's creation of the world and of working in wood. As many as four men in turn would set about carving decorations on a walking-stick, or take turns in carving stools or chairs; thus there could be no overall preconceived design. The ultimate criterion was whether it turned out well.

Thus Bohannan concluded that 'in Tivland almost every man is a critic. Because there are no specialists in taste and only a few in the manufacture of art, every man is free to know what he likes and to make it if he can. It seems to me that as many Tiv are aware of why they like something as are aware of the implications of any other aspects of their culture. In all spheres, this is a faculty which varies greatly from person to person.'

Most of the specialized studies of African art in the field have been conducted in societies which have professional artists, and have taken the artist and his creativity as the starting-point of the study. Thus Bohannan's account of the Tiv opened our eyes to other possibilities. There are indeed many societies in which, as among the Tiv, every man is his own artist. Among the Fanti and many Ibo groups art is fundamentally non-professional, though on occasion a man whose talent is well known may be commissioned to do work for someone else. In general, no prestige is attached to the work as the expression of an individual artist.[182] Yet there are also societies, such as the Yoruba, in which sculpture is usually a strictly professional affair, where the profession, and by implication the talent, usually runs in families. The casual attitude to art of the Tiv which Bohannan described is clearly impossible in societies where the art is the work of professional artists. Indeed, it seems likely that art produced by professionals may be less susceptible to outside stylistic influence than is the art of societies without a professional tradition.[183]

THE INDIVIDUAL ARTIST

One of the most exciting developments in recent years has been the demonstration that, in the societies which do have a professional tradition, individual artists are able to evolve their personal style within the sculptural tradition of the society. These personal styles can be identified and very often the artist can be named. Over the years connoisseurship in African sculpture has progressed from the identification of tribal styles through that of sub-tribal styles to that

222

of town or village styles, and finally reached the level of the style of the individual artist. We are even beginning to distinguish between the hands of masters and apprentices in the same workshop and to trace the development of the artist's style from his apprenticeship through to full mastery and even to decline.

The first style to be generally acknowledged as an individual one, though it is still not certain whether it should not rather be considered the style of a workshop, is the 'long-faced style of Buli'. Almost a *Ill. 218* score of pieces in this style are known but the place where they were collected has been recorded for only two of them: Buli. Even this is ambiguous for it is the name of a district as well as of a village, within the area occupied by the BaLuba.[184] The naming of this style by

218 Chief's stool from the BaLuba, carved in the 'long-faced style of Buli', the first style of an individual sculptor or workshop to be recognized. This unusual style contrasts strongly with that of more typical BaLuba pieces such as *Ills. 219–22*. British Museum. Ht 21 in.

219, 220 BaLuba neckrest with two caryatid figures with elaborate coiffures of the type which necessitates the use of such a device. The slight degree of asymmetry produced by the arms is particularly well handled. British Museum. Ht 6½ in.

221 Statue of a female ancestor, BaLuba. The rounded and smooth forms are typical of most BaLuba sculptures. British Museum. Ht $17\frac{1}{2}$ in.

222 Ivory neckrest, BaLuba. Formerly in the collection of Charles Ratton. Ht 7 in.

Olbrechts in 1938 represented a major breakthrough, even though the sculptor's name was not recorded. By now, the number of artists' names recorded in the published literature runs to many scores if not to hundreds. For example, the names of twenty-five carvers are mentioned from four quite small Nigerian groups in a short study by Roy Sieber.[185] Among the Montol he found that the carver's name is kept secret for masks which are still in use, though the name could be revealed when the mask ceased to be used.[186] The recording of artists' names and the identification of their works was pioneered by Kenneth Murray in Nigeria from the 1930s onwards. Most of his data is recorded in the files of the Department of Antiquities in Lagos and has thus not had the publicity it deserves. William Fagg has sought out artists and their works all over western Nigeria and elsewhere, and his writings abound with the names of individual sculptors and illustrations of their works.

One of the most detailed studies of individual artists, however, was conducted by Fischer among the Dan in north-eastern Liberia.[187] He studied the techniques and personalities of the sculptors Tame, Si, Tompieme and Sōn. By diagrams and photographs he shows that although their tools are similar, they use them in different ways; he shows too how the individual's style changes with time as his technique develops. Moreover, the sculptor may follow different methods with different types of mask. Tame carves a *geangle* mask (the upper part of the face of which has human features but the lower part resembles the bill of a bird) from a cylindrical block with a flattened

Ill. 223 back. Using an adze[188] he first cuts in deeply beneath the nose and blocks out the form of the bird-like bill. Then he cuts two horizontal grooves, above and below the eyes, and two sloping grooves to define the nose. He then cuts away the cheeks, and blocks out the forehead and the eyes. Only when the essential forms are visible on the front does he turn the mask over and hollow out the back. The work is finished with a knife. In making a *ngede* mask which has a

Ill. 224 human face, he first of all cuts the block of wood into an oval, the outline of the mask, and then cuts four grooves across the face converging towards the sides of the mask. These define the mouth, nose, eyes, forehead and hair. On the back he cuts a groove all round, parallel to the edge of the mask, with a transverse groove towards the top. He then hollows out the back of the mask, first the lower part, then the upper. Without completing the inside he turns the mask,

226

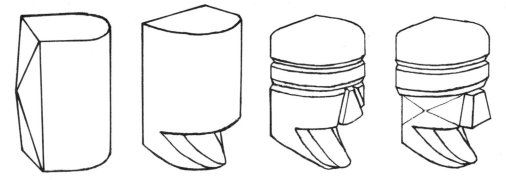

223 Stages in Tame's carving of a *geangle* mask. Dan. (After Fischer.)

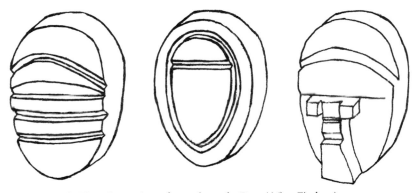

224 Stages in Tame's carving of a *ngede* mask. Dan. (After Fischer.)

over and reduces the main forms of the mask to a series of blocks, still using the adze. He even reduces the eyes from cubes to cylinders with this tool. Then he smoothes the surface and starts the eye holes with a knife, and then completes the adzing out of the back and, with a knife again, the piercing of the eyes. Aluminium teeth and eye rings are fitted and finally the mask is oiled.

In carving a *dea* mask (similar to *Ill. 174*) Tompieme shapes the outline of the face with his adze. On the back he cuts a groove across the upper part, stopping short of the edges of the mask. He strikes blows towards it from all directions, so that the chips of wood terminate at the groove. He takes out about two centimetres of wood

227

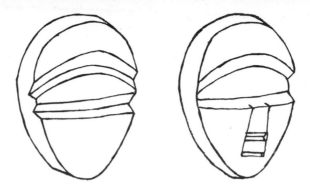

225 Stages in Tompieme's carving of a *dea* mask. Dan. (After Fischer.)

in this way, then turns the block over and cuts two grooves in the front, above and below the eyes, and immediately cuts back the area between. Taking a chisel, and using the haft of an adze as a mallet, he marks the outline of the nose, and proceeds to adze out the cheeks, leaving the nose and mouth as blocks. He separates the forehead and hair with the adze, then completes the detail with his knife, which he uses like a chisel, tapping the back of the blade with a block of wood to cut the grooves of the hair-dressing.

Fischer describes the techniques of the other carvers too, in far greater detail than is possible here, and it is clear that each one of them uses his tools in his own way. Sōn, for example, uses a gouge to hollow out the back of his masks, though he uses the adze on the front.

Father Kevin Carroll has worked closely with a group of Yoruba sculptors in a scheme which will be described in the last chapter. He has worked with carvers of several generations. Arowogun (born 1880, died 1954); his son Bandele (born about 1910) who was apprenticed not to his own father but to Oshamuko (died about 1945) who had himself been apprenticed to Arowogun; and Lamidi, the son of Fakeye (born about 1925) who was an apprentice of Bandele. Father Carroll has written the biographies of these three carvers[189] who all work in the style of the Yoruba town of Osi Ekiti. Lamidi is descended from a family of carvers who lived at Ila and was trained in the family style. He was not, however, a willing apprentice, though eventually, after five years with his father, he set up on his own in the town of Oro. Eventually he met Father Carroll and Bandele there and he was invited to become Bandele's apprentice. He was apprenticed for three years, during which he learned to carve in a different style, that of

228

Osi. His work during this apprenticeship is often very difficult to distinguish from that of his master, especially in door panels, though his sculpture in the round (masks and houseposts) is usually distinguishable.

One of the most popular subjects of Yoruba sculpture is the mounted warrior. *Ills. 226* to *229* show how the subject was treated by the sculptors we have just mentioned. The warrior is not usually represented alone when he is carved in a door panel, but is surrounded by other figures who complete the design and reduce the open space to a minimum, producing a richness of design which falls short of being overcrowded. Arowogun's style is characterized by relatively *Ill. 226* low relief with well-smoothed forms; the mouth is set low and the line of the jaw forms approximately a right angle with the line of the profile of the lips and nose; this line sweeps smoothly back to form the forehead; the eyes are carved very flatly and wide open. The panel by his apprentice Oshamuko is much less smooth and although *Ill. 227* it has been cut away and remounted, presumably when it was moved to a narrower doorway, there is a greater verticality to the design; the profile of the face is less regular than Arowogun's, and though the eyes are similar in shape, their form is more bulging. (Note the prisoner tied to the warrior's reins but represented floating over the horse's head.) Bandele's style is best characterized as bold. He has a *Ill. 228* remarkable motor skill in carving which Oshamuko also possessed: he is completely ambidextrous, a skill which saves considerable time and movement. Father Carroll remarks that 'it is quite uncanny to watch Bandele cut the delicate curve of an eyelid with one hand and then change the knife to his left hand to cut the opposite curve with equal precision and firmness'.[190] Clearly this ability makes him a very confident carver, whose work in relief is often marked by great depth of cutting so that the figures sometimes are almost carved in the round, as in this example. *Ill. 229* shows a detail of one of Lamidi's doors, part of a commission executed during his apprenticeship. It is one of a set carved for the rear gatehouse of the Palace in Ife.

It is very difficult to tell which doors are by Bandele and which by Lamidi, apart from the slightly greater depth of Bandele's carving. The ridge over the forehead, often continuing round the eye socket, is found in both, and the facial profiles and ear forms are also similar. In this particular example the prisoner appears to be standing on the horse's head.

226 Panel from a door carved by Arowogun. Nigerian Museum, Lagos. W. 25 in.

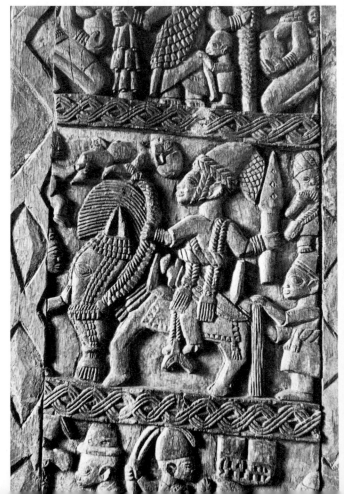

227 Panel from a door carved by Oshamuko, former apprentice of Arowogun. Nigerian Museum, Lagos. Ht of panel: $14\frac{1}{4}$ in.

228 Detail from a panel carved by Bandele, son of Arowogun and former apprentice of Oshamuko. Nigerian Museum, Lagos. W. 26½ in.

229 Panel from a door by Lamidi, son of Fakeye, former apprentice of Bandele. Idena gatehouse of the Palace of the Oni of Ife. W. 29 in.

Another carver of great individuality is Olowe of Ise (died 1938),
Ill. 230 who is probably the greatest Yoruba virtuoso sculptor. His figures
lean out from the door, the upper part being carved fully in the
round. His horsemen in this example are a district officer, said locally
to represent Captain Ambrose, who was Travelling Commissioner
for the Ondo Province in 1897, and his assistant, Reeve Tucker.[191]
Olowe had a great reputation. He was commissioned to carve doors
and pillars for several palaces of Yoruba kings. One door, thought
to be by him, still stands in the Palace in Ilesha, fifty miles away from
his home town. The top panel of this shows palm-wine tappers

230 Part of a door carved by the virtuoso Yoruba
sculptor, Olowe, representing Captain Ambrose
on tour, about 1897. His companion is said to be
Reeve Tucker. Nigerian Museum, Lagos. W.
22 in.

231 Pair of doors carved about 1910 by Olowe
for the Palace of the Ogoga of Ikere, showing
Captain Ambrose in a litter with his retinue being
received by the Ogoga wearing his beaded crown
and flanked by his attendants and wives. The
degree to which Olowe's figures are carved free
of the background is indicated by the broken
figure at the bottom right. British Museum. Ht
approx. 6 ft.

climbing trees which almost grow out of the background. His fame was even more widespread, for it was a pair of doors carved by him about 1910 for the King of Ikere which were sent for display at the British Empire Exhibition at Wembley in 1924 and are now in the British Museum. In his usual high-relief style he portrays the same British administrator, Mr Ambrose, in a litter, being received by the King of Ikere. Another *tour de force* by Olowe is shown in *Ill. 232*, for the head between the legs of the supporting figures is cut completely free, a device more commonly found in Chinese or Indian sculpture.

232 An elaborate bowl carved about 1925 by Olowe. The head between the supporting figures is completely separate from the rest of the sculpture. Coll. William J. Moore. Ht 25 in.

When I visited Lamidi early in 1960, he had become a master himself and already had four apprentices working with him, preparing for a big exhibition to be held in Ibadan in March and they were all busy making small carvings for which he could be assured of a ready sale. I was interested to discover how closely the style of his apprentices' work resembled his. He had carved a twin figure as a model for them to copy, and between them they had made fifty or sixty of them. I asked them to sort out those which each of them had carved and they did this quite easily. I then began to examine each group to see whether I could detect any consistency of individual style in the work of these relatively inexperienced artists. One of them, a nephew of Lamidi called Buraima Akinlabi Adewuyi had only just begun to carve and was still chiefly employed in completing the final stages of Lamidi's work. He had not carved any twin figures. Another, Amusa Akande, had come to work with Lamidi only three or four months earlier and had not yet developed his own style. The other two, however, had developed fairly marked styles, and I was quickly able to spot the one or two figures carved by the other apprentices which were in the wrong groups. The carvers were amazed that I could do this when they had failed to, though if they had taken more time no doubt they could have avoided the confusion. *Ill. 233* shows the piece which Lamidi carved as a model and one piece by each of the three apprentices which seemed most typical of their work. All four pieces show the facet on the chin running from the lower lip to merge into the flat undersurface of the chin, which is characteristic of Lamidi's figure sculpture. All have the ridge round the eyes and across the forehead, though this has been rounded off on Lamidi's and Joseph Fakeye's work. The ears are alike in all. All of them, however, have broader and shorter faces than their master's piece and none of them has the near-vertical lip surface which is characteristic of Lamidi's sculpture. The piece on the right of *Ill. 233* is by Ganiyu Fakeye, a nephew of Lamidi. The breasts on his female figures are conical and less bulbous than Lamidi's; the pubic hair on the female figures is very prominent and angular and extends to the hips; his male figures have a pointed penis; none of his figures have tribal scarification. The second figure from the left in *Ill. 233* is by Joseph Fakeye, another nephew of Lamidi. This carver stays close to his master's style, though the breasts of his figures are less bulbous and are truncated at the tip. He is the only carver to represent abdominal scarifications. The third figure in *Ill. 233* is by Amusa Akande; although his style was more variable than Ganiyu's or Joseph's, he was the only one to retain the charms round the neck; the form of the breasts is closest to Lamidi's, yet he has treated the hair in a totally different way. It is evident that even within an apprenticeship system the young sculptor is not required to copy his master's work slavishly (although the Guro carver Bassi Abigan was taught by his master simply to copy what he did, cut for cut, without any idea what the sculpture was to be, but this seems to be an exceptional procedure.[192])

Father Carroll has described in detail the stages of sculpture in Ekiti and the role of the apprentice. First comes *ona lile* – blocking out the main forms with an axe or adze, then comes *aletunle* – working over the main forms and breaking them into smaller precise masses with adze or chisel, e.g. the forms of ears, hands and eyes; this is followed by *didon* – smoothing the forms, chiefly with knife or chisel; and finally *fifin* – cutting sharp detail such as hair, eyelids and pattern work.[193] The share of the apprentice in these stages seems to vary a little. 'Lamidi writes of two of his apprentices "they can finish the work perfectly when I have done the rough work".'[194] Bandele's apprentices, however, share in the rough work,[195] presumably removing the bark and only carving out the surplus wood after the master carver has indicated where to cut. The final stages of blocking out and the whole of the second stage are the responsibility of the master, for it is this which determines the overall form and proportions of the sculpture. The smoothing of the forms may be left almost entirely to the apprentices, whereas 'the final sharp cutting, *fifin*, is best done by the master'.[196] It appears that apprentices begin by helping with the more or less mechanical aspects of the work, and as their skill increases more and more is entrusted to them. This, of course, applies to large masks, doors and houseposts; when he has acquired sufficient skill the apprentice will make small pieces (like the twin figures in *Ill. 233*) entirely by himself. Indeed, in other Yoruba groups, such as Ijebu, where no large-scale sculptures are made nowadays, the apprentice learns by making spoons and similar small objects entirely by himself.[197] In comparing the features of the large sculptures from Ekiti, however, with a view to identifying the hand that made them, we can establish a hierarchy of importance, for the basic forms of the sculpture, being set by the master carver during

236

233 *Ibeji*, single figures of twins. On the left is the example carved by Lamidi, with copies by his apprentices Joseph Fakeye, Amusa Akande and Ganiyu Fakeye. Coll. F. Willett. Hts $12\frac{3}{4}$, $11\frac{7}{8}$, $11\frac{3}{8}$, $11\frac{1}{8}$ in.

ona lile and *aletunle* are likely to be more consistent than the details of finish which are often left to apprentices. Thanks to this principle Willett and Picton were able to resolve conflicts in attributions by local informants of ancestor shrine sculptures in Owo. It is important to be able to do this, for not infrequently the work of an inferior carver will be attributed by its owner to the hand of a more famous sculptor, either deliberately to impress with the more prestigious name or more probably because the name of the lesser carver has been forgotten.

As work on these problems of connoisseurship progresses we may be able in the case of a well-documented carver to trace the development of individual assistants through to their independence as masters. African art is, in short, susceptible to the analytical techniques employed in the study of the more familiar traditions, for it too is art, no less than is Western and Oriental art.

234 Islam has not completely eliminated the representation of animals and human beings. These pottery sculptures were bought in the market at Mbour, south of Dakar, Senegal. Coll. F. Willett. Hts $4\frac{1}{4}$, $5\frac{3}{8}$ in.

CHAPTER SEVEN

African Art Today

When writing about traditional African art it is customary to write in the present tense without repeatedly indicating that only one point in time is being described. In consequence the idea has arisen that African art was unchanging until the relatively recent impact of outside influences such as Islam, and European traders and missionaries. In Chapter Three it was shown that African art has always been subject to change, but our knowledge is still too sketchy for us to make reliable assessments of rates of change. Nevertheless, it does appear that the rate has accelerated during the present century, due to the ever-increasing influx of Western ideas and technology. The passing of the old African ways of life have been much regretted by Western writers (though hardly at all by Africans) and the decline in the production of traditional art in particular has been greatly bemoaned. Yet there is so much artistic production still going on in Africa, in greater variety than before, that it seems likely that posterity will judge the second half of the twentieth century to have been a period of artistic renaissance for Africa as a whole.

External influences have been affecting Africa for a long time. One of the best documented of these is Islam which has been so long established in North Africa, across the Sudan savanna, in the Horn and along the east coast that it must be regarded as a traditional way of life in these areas, which at the same time belong also to the Muslim world as a whole. In general this is true also of their art, since Islam discourages the representation of living creatures and encourages instead elaborate ornamental designs. Yet we can find many Muslim peoples in Africa whose art is not entirely non-representational. The Nupe of northern Nigeria are best known nowadays for their chased brasswork, which is covered with intricate but non-representational

235 Detail of a door carved by Sakiwa the Younger of Lapai, in a house in the Nupe town of Lapai.

designs.[198] Their doors, although essentially ornamental, often include *Ill. 235* animals, while masked dancers are still active in Nupeland,[199] as they *Ill. 236* are among other Islamized peoples in West Africa. Labelle Prussin has shown how the Islamic mosque was made distinctively African[200] while Roy Sieber has shown that the Ashanti *kuduo*, a bronze vessel *Ill. 237* used to hold offerings at funerals and other rituals, has been developed from canteens of separate vessels fitting together, imported from the Arab world.[201] Previously it had been regarded as characteristically Ashanti. Thus not only did Islam not obliterate representational art, but it led in some respects to new creativity. Even where, as on the East African coast, Islamic ornament did not encounter a pre-existing representational tradition, its production deserves serious study. Figure sculpture may be absent from most of East Africa, but ornamental sculpture of great beauty is found.[202]

236 Mask collected at Mokwa by Frobenius in 1910. Islam has still not driven out the traditional Nupe masquerades though they only perform nowadays on the Prophet's Birthday. British Museum. Ht 25¾ in.

237 Bronze *kuduo*, Ashanti. The relief lines round it are skeuomorphic decorations derived from a prototype which consisted of separate vessels fitted together. British Museum. Ht 11 in.

238 Statue of Our Lady in the centre of the fishing village of Fadioute, Senegal, carved by Laurent Ndonc.

239 Nail fetish called *mangaka* from Loango, BaVili subdivision of the Ba-Kongo, collected about 1898. Nails are driven into such figures to obtain supernatural aid. Manchester Museum. Ht 46½ in.

240 Christian influence on African sculpture has shown itself in a variety of ways as in these angels, the male one being conceived as a government messenger with his pith-helmet, wristwatch and despatch-bag secured by his belt. Manchester Museum. Hts $16\frac{3}{4}$, $16\frac{3}{8}$ in.

Christianity has existed in Africa even longer than Islam, for Coptic Christianity in Egypt and Ethiopia goes back almost to the time of Christ himself, while Nubia was Christian from the sixth century, being Islamized only in the early seventeenth century. What ideas and artistic motifs may have been transmitted to the rest of contemporary Africa we do not yet know. Elsewhere sporadic attempts at proselytization were made by European missionaries on the west coast from the fifteenth century onwards. The most substantial result was the establishment of the Portuguese-speaking

244

Christian Kingdom of Kongo, which reached its height in the sixteenth century, but after a war with Portugal in 1665 Christianity faded away. The period, however, has left its mark in a number of locally made crucifixes and in the rock paintings at Mbafu. It is *Ill. 36* possible too that the emphatic naturalism of BaKongo sculpture may be due to European influence, but I cannot go so far as one of my colleagues who believes that the typical mother and child figure is a *Ill. 241* copy of the Madonna of the Humility, and that the *konde* nail fetish *Ill. 239* is derived from the crucified Christ.[203]

In general, Christian missionaries, even up to the present day, have been culpably ignorant of indigenous African religions and in attempting to undermine them have often attacked the sculptures which gave expression to their ideas, in the mistaken belief that they were idols and the object of worship. Gods indeed seem scarcely ever

241 Ancestor figure in the form of a squatting mother holding a child. BaKongo. Coll. Pierre Arman. Musée de l'Homme, Paris. Ht 12¼ in.

to be represented in African sculpture. Fortunately, oecumenism is beginning to embrace even traditional African religions and attempts are being made to utilize traditional art forms for Christian worship. It is interesting to see how the attitude of the secular administration has been reflected even in this unlikely context. French administration attempted to make its African subjects into Frenchmen, and this attitude, that European standards represent the pinnacle to which Africans should aspire, is reflected in five or six statues in the fishing *Ill. 238* village of Fadioute on the coast of Senegal. They were carved by Laurent Ndonc during the 1950s, all clearly in imitation of European plaster images of saints.

246

242, 243 Two *epa* masks carved by Bangboye of Odo Owa. Traditional carvers achieved perfection by repeatedly carving the same subject. The older example, collected in Oyate village, was called *Omoboni* and represents someone who has lived to see his own great-great-grandchildren. The younger example is said to have been collected at Odo Owa, but is not otherwise documented. Nigerian Museum, Lagos. Hts $42\frac{1}{2}$, $46\frac{1}{2}$ in.

Lord Lugard's policy of indirect rule – forwarding British policy through the existing traditional chiefs and institutions – could well have been the unconscious model for the Oye Ekiti project of a group of S.M.A. fathers in Nigeria. Father Kevin Carroll has described the sculptural aspects of the scheme.[204] The idea was to establish a centre of craftsmen who would employ the traditional forms of sculpture, weaving, embroidery, leather- and bead-work to help in the worship of the Christian God. The scheme was closed down after a few experimental years, but Fathers Carroll and O'Mahoney continued to encourage a number of sculptors who had been involved, particularly Bandele and Lamidi.

247

A typical product of the centre is shown in *Ill. 244*: a magus for a set of crib figures, carved by Lamidi and completed by other craftsmen. No attempt was made to convert the artists to Christianity and indeed the missionaries were even prepared to allow the carvers to undertake commissions for traditional cults. I well remember visiting an Ogboni house in Ekiti with Father Carroll in 1959 and seeing two drums which had been carved by Bandele while he was working

Ill. 246 with the scheme. The mandorla round the head is traditional on these drums and usually wider than here, as in the nineteenth-century

Ill. 245 example, and it has been turned to good account in Christian carvings

Ill. 247 such as on the font which Bandele carved in 1965.

244 One of the Three Wise Men from a crib scene, conceived as a Yoruba king with his beaded crown. Danford Collection, Birmingham University. Ht 22 in.

246 Two drums carved by Bandele for an Ogboni house in Ekiti. Ht *c.* 36 in.

245 Drum from an Ogboni house carved in the style of Osi Ekiti. Collected in the nineteenth century. Museum of Marischal College, Aberdeen. Ht 46 in.

247 Baptismal font carved by Bandele in 1965. The traditional mandorla seen on the preceding drums is here entirely in harmony with the figure of the risen Christ.

248 Untitled beadwork picture on cloth by Jimoh Buraimoh of Oshogbo.

His apprentice Lamidi is probably the best known of the Oye Ekiti carvers. Among other works he has carved many doors for public buildings which often portray scenes both from traditional Yoruba life and from the Bible. On the doors for the University College Hospital in Ibadan, carved in 1960, he represented also scenes in a modern hospital. All three types of subject harmonize well.[205]

With these new themes the artist is often attempting the subject for the first time, whereas he has repeatedly carved the traditional motifs and has already solved his main artistic problems. Lamidi is often asked to produce something new, since uniqueness is a value by which Westerners set much store. In consequence he and his apprentices do not get the opportunity to perfect their ideas and designs by repeating them at frequent intervals. It was this repetition with slight variations which ensured the certainty of touch of the old

249 'Leopard in a Cornfield', silkscreen print by Bruce Onobrakpeya, 1965. Coll. F. Willett. Ht 23¾ in.

African masters, for as we have mentioned, the African sculptor uses no sketch-book to practise in: his practice is in the finished sculpture.

The visual presentation of the Biblical stories in Christian churches, which was the primary aim of the Oye Ekiti scheme, corresponds very closely to the way in which sculptures, paintings, and stained glass in the European churches of the Middle Ages served both to inspire Christian sentiments in the worshippers and to instruct those members of the congregation who could not read. The Oye Ekiti scheme, however, attempted to go further and instituted ceremonies which employed these Christian images in ways which resembled the pagan ones. At Christmas-time children carried Christian images in procession, an idea copied from a traditional festival in which the

250, 251 Panel representing the Crucifixion carved by Osagie Osifo, in 1961 for the Catholic Chapel of the University of Ibadan. Osifo, born in Benin, employs a frontality of design and a trefoil background, similar to those in the ancient bronze plaques for which Benin is famous. *Left:* Catholic Chapel, University of Ibadan. Ht 32 in. *Right:* British Museum. Ht 19 in.

images are paraded round the town in celebrating a general benediction on the community. This is quite distinct from the cults which use masks.

But the Oye Ekiti carvers with their traditional training are not the only ones who are trying to supply a new religious basis for African art. Many of the artists who have received Western-type training in the art departments of both African and European colleges and universities are committed Christians. Their training has opened their horizons to all the art traditions of the world, so that they can be as eclectic as they wish, though they often show a preference for African models, as in Osifo's Crucifixion, which is organized after the example of a Benin plaque. In contrast Ben Enwonwu's doors for

Ills. 250, 251

253

Ill. 252

the Apostolic Delegation in Lagos are perhaps more Western than African in conception. There are a great many Western-trained artists practising in Africa,[206] but until recently they have had to work either for a Western public or on commissions from public institutions, largely because they ask prices for their work which are in keeping with the international art market, rather than geared to the average African income, a practice which Cyprian Ekwensi has criticized.[207] However, one artist at least, Bruce Onobrakpeya, has set the prices of some of his work low enough to attract African buyers, for if Western-trained artists are to remain truly African they must satisfy the artistic needs of their own society. Onobrakpeya's

Ill. 249

work, though often African in subject, is not particularly African in style. Western-trained African artists are going through a stage of very varied experimentation, stimulated by the art traditions of the other continents, rather as European artists were stimulated by African and Oceanic art at the beginning of this century. Their art is in consequence extremely individual, and often no more clearly African than is some of, say, Picasso's work. African artists are thus at present being absorbed into the cosmopolitan world of modern art, which owes its character mainly to the stimulus of traditional African art. The wheel has come full circle. Perhaps with the increasingly rapid communication of visual images, the Western-trained artists will continue to be eclectic and to play this role on the twentieth-century art scene, where regional distinctions seem no longer to be important. Perhaps, however, in time, they will turn more and more to the artistic traditions of their ancestors and perhaps begin to look increasingly to their own people for patronage. If they do, we may expect new African forms of art to emerge.

New forms of distinctively African art are in fact already emerging in several parts of Africa, where experimental centres have been established in which people, usually with no artistic training, can have the materials and opportunity to express themselves. The first was established about 1957 at Salisbury in Rhodesia by Frank McEwen, then Director of the National Art Gallery. There was no living tradition of sculpture or painting in the area when he began by supplying painting materials to the art gallery attendants. From this there rapidly developed a workshop from which some seventy artists all over Rhodesia have drawn encouragement. McEwen claims that his method is not to instruct these artists but to draw out their

252 Door of the chapel of the Apostolic Delegation, Lagos carved by Ben Enwonwu in 1965. Enwonwu was probably the first Western-trained African artist to win international fame.

'spirit of art'[208] by sympathy and encouragement. Most of these artists have taken to sculpture in hard stone which is well smoothed and then oiled. The use of such intractable material discourages the mass-production which has led to 'airport art' (a term which McEwen coined) which is identical wherever in Africa – or outside – one buys it. Yet this slowness of production is not necessarily a virtue if the end-product has similar qualities. Airport art is smooth and shiny to harmonize with European sitting-room furniture and some of the Salisbury work has a similar surface coupled with a naivety of vision which passes as 'truly African' with some of the unconsciously patronizing purchasers. Some of the work, however, is of very high quality – one could not expect all of it to be. McEwen insists that the artists are free to express their own ideas, uninfluenced by him. They do, however, influence each other and different carvers have produced very similar works.[209] If they did not influence each other, they could hardly have become a 'school'. Nevertheless, there is a good deal of variety in their work, most apparent when they work in soft stone. The Salisbury school has been operating for over a decade, but its only customers so far have been white. Now that McEwen has retired and no longer lives in Salisbury, we must wait to see how viable the school will be and whether it can develop an African patronage. Certainly McEwen's enterprise in 'trying to create new artists in the cultural desert of Rhodesia', as Beier described it,[210] deserves to be successful.

Ill. 253

253 'Entwined Figure', carved in soapstone by Nicholas Mukomberanwa of the Salisbury school, Rhodesia.

254 The Anti-bird Ghost, a black ink drawing on green-blue paper, by Twins Seven Seven, 1967. Coll. Edward Garrison. Ht 25 in.

A younger experiment inspired by Ulli Beier has already won for itself a certain amount of African patronage. This began as a series of summer schools, the first two of which, held in Ibadan in 1961 and 1962, were primarily for practising artists and art teachers, and aimed at freeing them from the inhibitions acquired during their Western type of training. Later in 1962 a similar school was organized at Mbari Mbayo, the artists' club in Oshogbo, and others were held in 1963 and 1964. They were open to anybody who cared to drop in. The participants were encouraged to experiment with a variety of media, and many continued to practise on their own, often relying on Beier for support.

The pictures produced by the Mbari artists such as Taiwo Olaniyi, who is also a night-club entertainer (drummer and dancer) under the name of Twins Seven Seven, often illustrate spirit figures from Amos *Ill. 254*

257

255, 256 Bronze castings from Old Obo made by an unknown artist for the cult of *egbe imole*: The man smoking his pipe is 6¼ in. tall, the horseman 7¼ in.

Tutuola's novels.[211] This literary approach, a tendency to represent figures from traditional folk-tales, is characteristic of present-day African art. It is very conspicuous for example in modern MaKonde sculpture,[212] but also in work made by traditional artists for sale to Europeans.

Another young man whose creativity was sparked off by the Mbari summer school is Jimoh Buraimoh. He has developed a technique of picture-making by sewing threaded beads on to cloth – a traditional Yoruba practice for objects to be used by the king. Now he is using epoxy resin adhesives to mount his beads on boards. He makes very effective use of bold masses of strong colour;[213] his engravings, in contrast, are composed of very fine lines and illustrate mythical creatures.

Ill. 248

The Mbari school of artists consists not only of these and other untrained artists, who discovered their undeveloped talents in the summer school, but of a number of other craftsmen who were encouraged by Ulli Beier and Susanne Wenger to develop themselves artistically long before the summer schools were started. The first of these to make a name for himself was Yemi Bisiri, a brass-smith trained in the tradition of Obo-Ekiti, to which style he has remained faithful.[214] His originality lies in making his castings larger than is usual nowadays in the style, for his figures are commonly fifteen inches high, twice as big as those now being made in Obo, though there are older pieces which are larger. Bisiri continues to work also for the local Ogboni Society, which is one of the principal traditional patrons of the brass-smith.

Ill. 257

Ills. 255–56

257 Mother with children cast in the Obo style by Yemi Bisiri of Ilobu. Coll. Ulli Beier. Ht 15 in.

258 Repoussé aluminium panel representing scenes from Yoruba life by Ashiru Olatunde of Oshogbo. Institute of African Studies, University of Ibadan. Ht $57\frac{1}{2}$ in.

259 Part of the Oshun shrine at Oshogbo refurbished by Susanne Wenger and local craftsmen. The undulating lines are intended to echo the movement of the River Oshun.

Another professional craftsman is Ashiru Olatunde who was having a hard time making a living out of sheet-copper ear-rings, which could not compete with cheap imports. Soon he was making small table ornaments a few inches high. Under Beier's encouragement he gradually increased the size of his products up to as much as three feet, while in 1966 he was commissioned to make doors for a *Ill. 258* church in Oshogbo.[215]

Susanne Wenger and Beier had been living in Oshogbo for some time before they began to seek out local talent. Susanne had been experimenting with her silk-screen prints and resist-dyed *adire* cloths, representing African myths and legends in her own angular style. She had become an Obatala priestess and had undertaken the decoration of a number of shrines in Oshogbo with pierced wooden screens of her own design. Still later she began to experiment with cement sculpture, at which point local people began to get involved. One of her projects was the refurbishing of the grove for Oshun, the great

261

260 Pierced cement screen round the Esso petrol station in Oshogbo by Adebisi Akanji. Palm-wine drinkers, dancers and drummers are shown.

261 Detail of the encircling wall of the Oshun shrine in Oshogbo, showing a sacrificial cow carved in low relief by Adebisi Akanji.

river goddess of Oshogbo. She designed the attractive free form sculptured building whose undulating lines in mud, rendered with cement, echo the movement of the river, but she got local masons to decorate the walls which surround the most sacred area. The entrance gate was decorated by Adebisi Akanji, the most talented of them, who was already becoming well known as a result of Beier's encouragement and had undertaken large-scale work already in cement sculpture.[216]

Ill. 259

Ill. 261

Adebisi was commissioned to decorate the Esso petrol station opposite the Mbari Mbayo Club in Oshogbo. His cement screens hide the standard glass hut found in all these filling stations behind lively representations not only of cars being filled (the driver of one of which is said to represent Susanne Wenger), but also of palm-wine drinkers, dancers and drummers.[217]

Ill. 260

Most of the artistic talent of the Mbari school has found expression in two dimensions. The rich tradition of sculpture in Nigeria seems to have inhibited them and made them prefer to leave sculpture to the professionally trained. Even the Western-trained artists have for the most part concentrated on painting rather than sculpture, though Idubor, Osifo and Enwonwu are outstanding exceptions.

The untrained artists of the Mbari group are interesting too as one of the few examples of an African phenomenon which can be compared to those instances of European folk-art in which the peasantry has developed an art style for its own use, based on the art of the landowning aristocracy.[218] It is particularly interesting that so many of the Mbari painters have drawn inspiration from the spirits in Amos Tutuola's novels,[219] for he too is a kind of folk-artist, in that he has had no formal training in writing.

What then is happening to art in Africa today? It is changing with the times as it always has done, but whereas the traditional artist drew on traditional forms to serve the needs of the community in which he lived – and this still continues in many areas – the Western-trained artist has the whole world on which to draw, and has still to find an adequate patronage within Africa. Yet groups of quite untrained artists are arising who, never having been separated from their communities during formal training, are able to serve the needs of their own areas. Perhaps it is to them that we should look for the future of specifically African art, while the Western-trained artists may well remain part of the cosmopolitan world of art. Many writers have bemoaned the sorry state and impending death of African art. Happily they are mistaken.

NOTES

BIBLIOGRAPHY

ACKNOWLEDGMENTS

INDEX

Notes

1 Population figures for Africa are highly unreliable. The figures used in the text have been made up purely for the purpose of illustration. When statistical studies of the type referred to below (p. 42) are more advanced we shall no doubt have figures about the art expressed in a comparable way.

2 This term applies to the whole belt of savanna which stretches right across Africa from East to West, just south of the Sahara. It should not be confused with the country of the same name which lies at its eastern end (the former Anglo-Egyptian Sudan) nor with the former French Sudan (now called Mali) towards its western end. The word comes from an Arabic phrase which means 'the country of the black people'. See *Ill. 25*.

3 For purposes of identification it is standardized practice never to quote a radiocarbon date without its laboratory number, which in this book is placed in parentheses, and its Standard Deviation which is an integral part of the date, expressing its statistical probability, i.e. there is a likelihood of two to one that the real date lies within the limits expressed; if the Standard Deviation is doubled the probability is increased to nineteen to one; while if it is trebled, the probability is 997 to 3, which is usually regarded as practical certainty: there are still however three chances in a thousand that the true date lies between these extended limits and the present day or the infinite past. Isolated radiocarbon dates therefore need to be viewed with caution and archaeologists nowadays attempt to obtain several dates from each period to ensure a conspectus. On the technique itself see Libby, 1952 and Barker, 1958.

4 See for example: F. Clark Howell, *Early Man*, Time Inc., New York, 1965, pp. 168–91.

5 See Nicholas England, Bushman Counterpoint, *Journal of the International Folk Music Council*, **19** (1967) pp. 58–66; Hukwe Bushmen, *Ethnomusicology*, **8**, No. 3 (1964) pp. 223–77, and also his recordings of *Bushman Music*, Nos. 1433 and 1433A, Musée de l'Homme/Peabody Museum. Colin Turnbull has published a recording of Pygmy music: *Music of the Ituri Forest People*, Folkways Records No. FE 4483.

See also G. Rouget and Y. Grimaud, *Notes on the Music of the Bushmen Compared to that of the Babinga Pygmies*, Phonodisc LD9, Musée de l'Homme/Peabody Museum.

6 Information from Professor Alan Jacobs.

7 See for example the pieces illustrated in L. Holy, 1967, in which one group, the MaKonde, is represented by twenty-seven pieces, while the next largest group of plates is seven or eight pieces from the Zulu. The MaKonde appear to have migrated from the Southern Congo basin and are agriculturists who grow cassava and do not keep cattle, whereas the Zulu have an economy evenly balanced between the cultivation of maize and animal husbandry (*Ills. 13, 14*).

8 The median is the measurement which represents the mid-point in the distribution of sizes, i.e. half the examples are larger and half are smaller. For the kind of comparison made in the text a simple mean (average) would give far too much weight to the isolated pieces of unusually large size.

9 Kevin Carroll, 1967, p. 91. This suggestion appears to be borne out by the Salisbury School in Rhodesia, where Frank McEwen encouraged potential artists in an area with no recent sculptural tradition, but where, within a few years, some works were being produced which were clearly better than the rest.

10 Paraphrased from Griaule, 1950, pp. 31–33.

11 Turnbull, 1961.

12 Griaule, 1950, p. 38.

13 By George W. Harley, 1941 and 1950.

14 Some social anthropologists however still retain the term 'primitive' in reference to the kind of small scale 'pre-literate' societies on the study of which their discipline was originally constructed. These societies are essentially self-sufficient, producing goods for their own consumption, not for export. The art of such societies is similarly produced for consumption within the societies, and hence can be considered the art of primitive societies, but it is the societies, not the art, which are 'primitive' in this

special sense. Similarly William Fagg's term 'tribal art' transfers the epithet from the society to the art. William Fagg tells me that Webster Plass pointed out that one of the meanings given by Samuel Johnson for 'primitive' is 'underived', and in this particular sense it might broadly be applied to these forms of art. In general usage however this meaning does not seem to survive.

15 Gottfried Semper, *Der Stil in den technischen und tektonischen Künsten, oder praktische Aesthetik*, Frankfurt and Stuttgart, 1861, 1863.

16 A bibliography of Holmes's writings (up to his seventieth birthday in 1916) was published in *Holmes Anniversary Volume*, Washington, 1916, pp. 491–99. His most important papers for our purpose appear in the *Annual Report of the Bureau of Ethnology* (Washington), **2** (1883), **3** (1884), **4** (1886), **6** (1888), **13** (1896), **20** (1903); *American Anthropologist*, **3** (1890), **5** (1892), n.s. **3** (1901) and *Proceedings of the American Association for the Advancement of Science, 1892* (Salem, 1892), *1893* (Salem, Massachusetts, 1894).

17 *Indianerstudien in Zentralbrasilien*, Berlin, 1905.

18 A. Gerbrands, 1957, p. 33. This is an invaluable study on which I have drawn extensively in the preparation of this chapter.

19 Evolution in the ornamental art of savage peoples, *Transactions of the Rochdale Literary and Scientific Society*, **3**, 1891 (translated from *Ymer*, 1890); *Collected Essays in Ornamental Art by Hjalmar·Stolpe*, translated by H. C. March, Stockholm, 1927.

20 *Decorative Art of British New Guinea*, Royal Irish Academy Cunningham Memoirs No. 10, Dublin, 1894; *Evolution in Art: as illustrated by the Life-Histories of Designs*, London, 1895.

21 *Papers by General Pitt-Rivers, Anthropological, Archaeological and other Contributions to learned Societies up to 1884*. Printed privately, London (Taunton Castle, Somerset), 1887–1903. *Evolution of Culture and Other Essays*, ed. J. L. Myres, Oxford, 1906.

22 *The Evolution of Decorative Art*, London, 1893.

23 *Abstraktion und Einfühlung*, Munich, 1908; *Abstraction and Empathy*, transl. Michael Bullock, New York, 1953. Worringer's ideas were summarized by T. E. Hulme in a lecture given in 1914 but not published till 1936: *Speculations*, ed. Herbert Read, London, 1936, pp. 75–109.

24 1953 ed., p. 13.

25 1953 ed., p. 54.

26 *Bulletin of the American Museum of Natural History*, **9**, pp. 123–76.

27 Cambridge, 1932.

28 London, 1960 and 1965.

29 Leipzig, 1915.

30 This was first observed by Robert Hottot in 1906. See p. 161.

31 It is often helpful in understanding other cultures to look for appropriate parallels in our own. Here we may compare the scene in Shakespeare's play in which Hamlet orders Horatio and Marcellus
'Never to speak of this that you have seen,
Swear by my sword.' (I. v.)
Here the sword being cruciform symbolizes the cross on which Christ died, and it is upon the cross that they are being asked to swear.

32 Frobenius, Die Kunst der Naturvölker [The Art of Native Peoples], *Westermanns Monatshefte* **79** (1896), pp. 329–40, 593–606; Die bildende Kunst der Afrikaner [Representational art of the Africans], *Mitteilungen der anthropologischen Gesellschaft in Wien*, **27** (1897), pp. 1–17: Die Masken und Geheimbünde Afrikas [The Masks and Secret Societies of Africa], *Abhandlungen der Kaiserlichen Leopoldinisch-Carolinischen Deutschen Akademie der Naturforscher*, **74** (1898), pp. 1–278.

33 See also Jean Laude, 1966, pp. 34–40; and the older study of R. J. Goldwater, *Primitivism in Modern Painting*, New York, 1938.

34 Available in French translations: *Les Arts Plastiques du Congo Belge*, Brussels and Amsterdam, 1959. A translation into English by Dan and Pearl Crawley, *Congolese Sculpture*, is to be published shortly.

35 This eventually led to the publication *Sculptures Soudanaises*, Paris, 1948, which was not very well translated as *Sudanese Sculptures*, Paris, 1949.

36 Gerbrands has since followed up this study with field-work of his own in New Guinea, described in *Wow-ipits, eight Asmat wood carvers of New Guinea* (The Hague, 1967) and in *Symbolism in the Art of Amanamkai, Asmat Southern New Guinea* (Leiden, Mededeelingen van het Rijksmuseum voor Volkenkunde **15**, 1962).

37 *Afrique Noire, La Création Plastique*, Paris, 1967.

38 *Classical African Sculpture*, London, 1954 and 1964.

39 Most conveniently described in Griaule, 1950.

40 See Horton, 1966.

41 *Current Anthropology*, **10**, 1, 1969, pp. 3–44.

42 Anne-Marie Schweeger-Hefel, *Holzplastik in Afrika*, Vienna, 1960, analyses the stylistic features of some 930 African sculptures from several museums in an effort to provide a statistical basis for the definition of African art styles.

43 See Willett, 1967; Radiocarbon dates from Nigeria, *West African Archaeological Newsletter*, **9** (1968); New radiocarbon dates from Ife, *ibid.*, **11** (1969), pp. 23–25. On Benin chronology see

W. B. Fagg, 1963; R. E. Bradbury, Chronological problems in the study of Benin history, *Journal of the Historical Society of Nigeria*, **1**, 1959, pp. 263–87; and G. E. Connah, Radiocarbon dates for Benin City..., *Journal of the Historical Society of Nigeria*, **4**, 1968, pp. 313–20.

44 Griaule, 1950, p. 24.

45 Willcox, 1963, p. 1.

46 The most useful general sources on the Tassili art are Henri Lhote, 1959; The rock art of the Maghreb and the Sahara in Bandi *et al.*, 1961, pp. 99–152; and J. D. Lajoux, 1963.

47 Other dates from the Tassili are: Jabbaren II: 3520±300 BC (Sa-66); Initinen I: 2910±250 BC (Gif-286); Initinen II: 2680±250 BC (Gif-287); Titerast-n'-Elias 3: 2610±250 BC (Gif-288); Ekeham ouan Tartait 7: 2520±250 BC (Gif-292); Jabbaren I: 2320±300 BC (Sa-65). At Uan Muhuggiag in the Acacus, the Libyan extension of the Tassili, a sandstone block bearing part of a middle Cattle Period painting lay in a deposit dated 2770±310 BC (GX-87); the painting must be older than this date.

48 A technique of dating by the amino-acids in the paint is being developed in studying Bushman paintings. The technique looks promising but seems to be limited in its time-scale.

48a Paintings of round-headed figures at Uan Telocat in the Acacus have been reported to be older than 4804±290 BC (GX-88).

49 In this both forelegs are extended forwards and both rear legs backwards, whereas the earlier paintings show the natural gait of all the animals with the forelegs out of step with the rear.

50 Bandi *et al.*, 1961, p. 133.

51 See J. H. Greenberg, *The Languages of Africa*, Bloomington, 1963, pp. 7, 28–30, and G. P. Murdock, *Africa, its Peoples and their Culture History*, New York, 1959, p. 415.

52 Bernard Fagg, The cave paintings and rock gongs of Birnin Kudu (Northern Nigeria), *Proceedings of the Third Pan-African Congress on Prehistory*, London, 1957, pp. 306–12; The rock gong complex today and in prehistoric times, *Journal of the Historical Society of Nigeria*, **1** (1956), pp. 27–42; The discovery of multiple rock gongs in Nigeria, *Man*, **56** (1956), No. 23, and correspondence from various writers: *Man*, **56** (1956), No. 73, and **57** (1957), Nos. 32, 33, 34, 96, 142, 182, 250, 251; and J. H. Vaughan, Rock paintings and rock gongs among the Marghi of Nigeria, *Man*, **62**, 1962, No. 83.

53 e.g. by Holm in Bandi *et al.*, 1961, pp. 167–84.

54 1956, p. 70; 1963, pp. 49–50; 1968.

55 *Journal of African History*, **7** (1966), pp. 501–2.

56 Cf. J. R. Harding, Interpreting the 'White Lady' rock-paintings of South-West Africa: some considerations, *South African Archaeological Bulletin*, **23** (1968), pp. 31–34.

57 An examination of the Geji rock shelter in Nigeria showed that several styles overlapped each other but not in a consistent way. Apparently the different styles were in contemporary use. See H. Sassoon, Cave paintings recently discovered near Bauchi, Northern Nigeria, *Man*, **60** (1960), No. 70.

58 Willcox, 1956, p. 61.

59 On Bushman and related cave art see: Willcox, 1956; 1963; and 1968; J. D. Clark, *The Prehistory of Southern Africa*, Harmondsworth, 1959, pp. 253–80; The South African Archaeological Society, *Rock Paintings in Africa*, Cape Town, no date; and E. Goodall, C. K. Cooke, J. D. Clark and R. Summers, *Prehistoric Rock Art of the Federation of Rhodesia and Nyasaland*, Salisbury, 1959. References to older works will be found in Willcox, 1956, and 1963.

60 Information from D. W. Philipson, who is preparing a book on the rock art of Zambia. See also C. K. Cooke, Rock paintings and engravings of Africa, *Tarikh*, **1** (1966), No. 3, pp. 45–66; and M. Posnansky, *Prelude to East African History*, London, 1966, pp. 51–57.

61 G. Mortelmans and R. Monteyne, 1962.

62 See Allison, 1968a and b.

63 A useful general account of this site is Bernard Fagg, 1969. General accounts of the Nok Culture are: Bernard Fagg, 1956; 1959; and 1962. It is to be noted that the Stone Age remains from the original sites in the Nok area are now considered to belong to an earlier occupation, and that the Nok Culture is now regarded as fully of the Iron Age, not as transitional from the Late Stone Age to the Iron Age.

64 Allison, 1968a, pp. 21–24; and P. Stevens, The festival of the images at Esie, *Nigeria Magazine*, **87** (1965), pp. 236–43.

65 W. B. Fagg, 1959.

66 Allison, 1968a, pp. 36–41.

67 Dates from the layer in which these sculptures lay are: AD 1060±130 (BM-262) and AD 1150±200 (M-2119). Taken with the dates from below pavements which appear to have been contemporary with the one beside which these sculptures lay, AD 960±130 (BM-261) and AD 1160±130 (BM-259) we may infer a twelfth-century date for the deposit.

68 This site is called Orun Oba Ado, and is the place where the heads of the kings of Benin were sent for burial: Pit XI AD 560±130 (BM-265); Pit III AD 800±120 (M-2114); Pit V AD 800±120 (M-2115); Pit VI AD 940±150 (M-2116) and AD 990±130 (BM-264).

269

69 AD 840±145 (I-1784); AD 840±110 (Hv-1515); AD 850±120 (I-2008); AD 875±130 (Hv-1514).

70 Bernard Fagg, 1962; and D.C. Simmonds, The depiction of gangosa on Efik-Ibibio masks, *Man*, **57** (1957), No. 18.

71 The history of Nigerian sculpture is discussed more fully in Willett, 1967. Other important sites in the history of sculpture are Igbo-Ukwu, described in Thurstan Shaw, 1970; Daima, described by Graham Connah in *Illustrated London News*, 14 October 1967, Archaeological Section 2276; *First Interim Report*, 1966, and *Second Interim Report*, Northern History Research Scheme, Zaria, 1967; *West African Archaeological Newsletter*, **3** (1965), **5** (1966), **6** (1967); and other sites around Lake Chad described by Lebeuf and Detourbet, 1950; and Lebeuf, 1951 and 1962. The Ilesha site has been described by Willett. Recent archaeological discoveries in Ilesha, *Odu*, **8** (1961), pp. 4–20. A detailed report *Excavations in the Royal Palace at Ilesha* is in preparation.

72 Excavations have been conducted in the caves from which these figures come. A preliminary account is: B.J. Bazuin-Sira, Cultural remains from the tellem caves, *West African Archaeological Newsletter*, **10**, pp. 14–15. See also J. Huizinga, New physical anthropological evidence bearing on the relationships between Dogon, Kurumba and the extinct West African Tellen populations, *Koninkl. Nederl. Akademie van Wettenschappen, Proceedings* Series C, **71**, No. 1 (1968), pp. 16–30.

73 See W.B. Fagg, 1963, Pls 54b, 55a and b.

74 A note on the Afro-Portuguese ivories, *Journal of African History*, **5** (1964), pp. 363–65.

75 *Esmereldo de Situ Orbis*, ed. R. Mauny, Bissau, 1956.

76 This system is still used by the Yoruba of Dahomey and Nigeria, and neighbouring peoples use related systems. The tray is dusted over with powdered wood or flour in which a pattern of marks is made to indicate whether one or two palm nuts remain in the left hand when the diviner attempts to pick up sixteen nuts with his right hand. A single short stroke is made if two nuts remain, a pair of strokes if one. This procedure is repeated four times, producing one of sixteen possible patterns in the dust on the tray. The pattern refers the diviner to the appropriate *odu* or section of the associated body of oral literature in which the answer is to be found. Repeating the procedure refers him to one of the sixteen subsections into which each major *odu* is divided. The diviner, who is kept in ignorance of the client's problem, recites the verses thus indicated while the client listens for one which answers his need. See William Bascom, 1969, and Bernard Maupoil, *La Géomancie à l'ancienne Côte des Esclaves*, Travaux et Mémoires de l'Institut d'Ethnologie, **42**, Paris, 1943.

77 Illustrated in Trowell, 1965, Pl. 58 centre.

78 Allison, 1968a, pp. 42–45.

79 The former is illustrated in Leuzinger, 1960, Pl. 30a, and 1963, Pls. 86a–d; the latter in William Fagg, 1951, Pl. 26.

80 Fagg, 1963, caption to fig. 111.

81 Von Luschan, 1919, tabulates 2400 pieces, the bulk of which were brought from Benin at the time of the Expedition. This total includes some items which are utilitarian rather than artistic.

82 For example, seven pieces which he illustrates in *Das unbekannte Afrika*, Munich, 1923 are described as having been 'excavated in Modakeke', which is part of Ife. In *Und Afrika Sprach*, Berlin, 1912, they are described as: 'from the grave of a Shango priest, Oyo'; 'from a grave near Offa'; 'from Yoruba temples'; two are said to be 'from the ruins of Old Oyo', while in two cases no provenance is given.

83 1935, II, p. 28.

84 M. Delafosse, *Haut-Sénégal-Niger*, Paris 1912, p. 200 calls them *griots*, which corresponds roughly to the English minstrel.

85 Quoted from *Ibn Battuta Travels in Asia and Africa*, translated by H.A.R. Gibb, London, 1929, p. 329.

86 ed. Mauny, 1956, p. 132.

87 p. 134.

88 p. 136.

89 p. 76.

90 Walter Hirschberg, *Schwarzafrika*, Graz, 1962, p. ★55. Most of the illustrations referred to in this chapter will be found in this book.

91 1919, fig. 515.

92 1903, p. 161.

93 Quoted from Ling Roth, 1903, p. 160.

94 A bronze snake head and other recent finds in the old palace at Benin, *Man*, **63** (1963), No. 174.

95 Quoted from Ling Roth, 1903, p. 162, following William Bosman's *Description of Guinea*, London, 1705.

96 The late Commander (Hugh) Clapperton, *Journal of a Second Expedition into the Interior of Africa from the Bight of Benin to Soccatoo*, London, 1829, p. 48.

97 F. Willett, Investigations at Old Oyo, 1956–57, an interim report, *Journal of the Historical Society of Nigeria*, **2** (1961), pp. 59–77.

98 William Allen, R.N., *Picturesque Views on the River Niger . . .*, London, 1840, p. 16 and facing plate.

99 William Fagg, 1963, pp. 30–39 and Pls 11 to 53. See also Forman and Dark, 1960.

100 W.J. Perry, *The Children of the Sun*, London, 1923, and *The Growth of Civilization*, London, 1924; and G. Elliot Smith, *Human History*, London, 1929.

101 1964, pp. 51, 52, 53, 62 and 83. Note also that she quotes Michael Sadler's assertion (*Arts of West Africa*, London, 1935, p. 54) that 'the two-faced mask' (of the Cross River area of southern Nigeria) 'inevitably recalls the two-faced Roman divinity Janus, from whom, in view of the ancient history of this region, in so far as it is known, it may be actually derived' (p. 67). Of the same area she writes on p. 43: 'It seems probable from specimens of bronze work found in the locality and other indications that Carthaginians established a trading post on the Cross River about 500 B.C.' Presumably she bases this inference on the piece from the Andoni Creeks illustrated in Underwood, 1949, Pl. 61, which is clearly a product of the Lower Niger Bronze Industries, and for the date of which there is as yet no evidence at all.

102 e.g. P. A. Talbot, *The Peoples of Southern Nigeria*, London, 1926, *passim*; C. K. Meek, *A Sudanese Kingdom*, London, 1931; E. L. R. Meyerowitz, *The Divine Kingship in Ghana and Ancient Egypt*, London, 1960. Robert G. Armstrong has published a valuable article on The development of Kingdoms in Negro Africa, *Journal of the Historical Society of Nigeria*, **2**, Pt I, pp. 27–39.

103 *Africa and Africans*, Garden City N.Y., 1964, pp. 81–82.

104 i.e. the figure faces foursquare to the front in a symmetrical pose.

105 This statement is modified from Cyril Aldred, *Old Kingdom Art in Ancient Egypt*, London, 1949, p. 1, where he draws a parallel with Polynesian practices.

106 *Ibid.*, pp. 1–3.

107 There is for example an Egyptian statuette found in Katanga in the southern Congo, published by R. Grauwet, in *La Revue Coloniale Belge*, IX (1954), No. 214, p. 622. How it got there is quite obscure. A.J. Arkell has also published Gold Coast copies of 5th-7th century [Egyptian] bronze lamps, *Antiquity*, **24** (1950), pp. 38–40.

108 See the article by L. Segy, The Ashanti Akua'ba statues as archetype, and the Egyptian Ankh: a theory of morphological assumptions, *Anthropos*, **58** (1963), pp. 839–67.

109 See for example the attempt by Archdeacon J. O. Lucas, *The Religion of the Yoruba*, Lagos, 1948, to show that the Yoruba language and religion, and hence the people themselves, are of Egyptian origin. Roger Westcott reviewed this book at length together with E. L. R. Meyerowitz's *The Divine Kingship in Ghana and Ancient Egypt*, London, 1960, in *The Journal of African History*, **2** (1961), pp. 311–

21. A collection of readings discussing the relations between Africa and Egypt will be found in Robert O. Collins, *Problems in Africa History*, Englewood Cliffs, N.J., 1968, pp. 7–55.

110 J.-P. Lebeuf, 1961.

111 M. Swithenbank, 1969.

112 J. Glück, 1957; H. Haselberger, 1964.

113 See M. W. Smith, ed., 1961, Pls XIIIc and d.

114 C. K. Meek, *Tribal Studies in Northern Nigeria*, London, 1931, vol. II, pp. 51–53 describes the Katab version of this type of house, providing a diagram which suggests that it is less refined than that of the Ham from which Meek suggests it was derived.

115 M. Trowell, 1960, Pl. I.

116 *Ibid.*, Pl. IX.

117 The building of these houses has been described and beautifully illustrated by Raymond Lecoq, 1953.

118 I am indebted to Mr J. C. Moughtim for information about this. His M.A.Arch. dissertation on Islamic architecture in northern Nigeria is kept at Liverpool University.

119 See Neville Chittick, Kilwa, *Azania*, I (1966), p. 20 and Pl. XI.

120 Illustrated in *Nigeria Magazine*, **30** (1949), pp. 304–5. Pp. 306–7 show china bowls and plates set in walls.

121 Prussin, 1968; 1970a and b.

122 Ojo, 1966, p. 97.

123 Glück is mistaken in referring to 'clay bricks'.

124 Information from Dr R. E. Bradbury. See also Akenzua, 1965.

125 A D 720 ± 120 (GX-347); A D 330 ± 90 (GX-348); A D 1445 ± 85 (GX-900); A D 1480 ± 110 (M-1892); A D 1650 ± 100 (M-1893); A D 1750 ± 100 (M-1894).

126 Margaret Trowell, 1964, p. 57.

127 *Ibid.*, p. 75.

128 P. S. Wingert, *Primitive Art, its Traditions and Styles*, Cleveland, 1965, p. vii.

129 *West Africa: Court and Tribal Art*, Arts Council, London, 1967, catalogue of an exhibition organized by William Fagg.

130 See for example his articles Bronze Age Technology in Western Asia and Northern Europe, *Man*, **58** (1958), Nos 13, 39 and 64.

131 Underwood, 1947, p. 41.

132 *Ibid.*, p. 42.

133 Shown in Berlin and Paris (Fagg, 1964) and later published with additional examples as Fagg, 1965 of which Fagg, 1966 is a condensed paperback version.

134 Paulme, 1962, p. 21.

135 Carroll, 1967, p. 94.

136 Horton, 1966, p. 21.

137 Frobenius's interpretation is mentioned on p. 35.

138 Hottot, 1956.

139 Fernandez, 1966, p. 59.

140 Herskovits, 1938, II, pp. 354–61.

141 Himmelheber, 1964, p. 255.

142 In M. W. Smith, 1961, p. 96.

143 Gerbrands, 1957, pp. 111–21.

144 The word 'fetish' has been much misused by writers about African art. It should refer only to objects either composed of or containing 'medicines' which have magical power in their own right.

145 See P. Morton-Williams, The Yoruba Ogboni cult in Oyo, Africa, **30** (1960), pp. 362–74.

146 Hottot, 1956, p. 34.

147 Horton, 1966, p. 13.

148 In M. W. Smith, 1951, p. 95.

149 African Writers Series, London, 1965, pp. 250–51.

150 Paulme, 1962, Pl. VI and p. 23.

151 Cf. Dominique Darbois, African Dance, Prague, 1962, pp. 71, 74–80.

152 Horton, 1966, p. 15.

153 Ibid., p. 12.

154 Ibid., p. 12.

155 Ibid., p. 14.

156 This account of Vandenhoute's work is derived from Gerbrands, 1957.

157 Himmelheber's most accessible account for English readers is his paper of 1964.

158 J. Girard, 1967.

159 Fagg, 1965, p. 11.

160 See Biebuyck, 1969, pp. 2–3.

161 Olbrechts, 1959, p. 26.

162 Reported and illustrated in Gerbrands, 1957, pp. 89–90 and Pls 4–7.

163 Olbrechts, 1959, pp. 47–48 and 81.

164 Letter to the author, 12 January 1967.

165 Vandenhoute, 1948, pp. 18–19.

166 Boston, 1960, p. 58.

167 Private communication to the author.

168 Himmelheber, 1935, pp. 72–74.

169 Gerbrands, 1957, Pls 4–7.

170 A Dan sub-group.

171 Another Dan sub-group.

172 A criterion which Picton found also among the Igbira.

173 Fischer, 1963, pp. 209–10.

174 Thompson, 1968, and more fully in a paper in The Traditional Artist in African Society, ed. W. d'Azevedo (in the press).

175 d'Azevedo, 1966, pp. 63–64.

176 Biebuyck, 1969, p. 17. This account follows Biebuyck's comments in this book and in D. Fraser and H. M. Cole, eds., The Arts of Leadership (in the press). It should be pointed out that the Bwami Society had been outlawed by the Belgian Government in 1933, then tolerated for a time, before again being outlawed in 1948. Biebuyck conducted his field-work in 1953–54, 1955 and 1958, so that some of his data may not truly reflect an earlier time.

177 Child and Siroto, 1965. The experiment was designed by Child and conducted in the field by Siroto.

178 Fernandez, 1966, p. 56.

179 Ibid., p. 55.

180 Loc. cit.

181 Artist and critic in an African society, in Smith, 1961, pp. 85–94.

182 K. C. Murray, The artist in Nigerian tribal society: a comment, in Smith, 1961, pp. 95–101.

183 Murray, loc. cit., p. 100.

184 Information from Professor Jan Vansina.

185 Sieber, 1961.

186 Ibid., p. 12.

187 Fischer, 1963.

188 A tool which resembles an axe but which has the cutting edge at right angles to the handle instead of being in the same plane.

189 Carroll, 1967, pp. 79–115.

190 Ibid., pp. 93–94.

191 Allison, 1944.

192 Himmelheber, 1935, pp. 17–18.

193 Carroll, 1967, p. 94.

194 Carroll, 1961.

195 Carroll, 1967, p. 94.

196 Ibid., pp. 94–95.

197 Cordwell, 1956.

198 Illustrated in Nigeria Magazine, **74** (1962), pp. 57–60.

199 Though Phillips Stevens informs me that at Mokwa the festival, called *elo*, is now performed only on the Prophet's birthday. For an earlier account of this and other cults see S.F. Nadel, *Nupe Religion*, London, 1954, especially pp. 214–16 and Pl. 28. Other Nupe masquerades are *Ndakogboza* and *Gugu*, illustrated in *Nigeria Magazine*, **50** (1956), pp. 275–77.

200 See pp. 120–127.

201 In a lecture to the African Studies Association, New York, October 1967.

202 See for example V. L. Grottanelli, Somali Wood Engraving, *African Arts*, **1**, No. 3, pp. 8–13, 72–73, and F. R. Barton, Zanzibar doors, *Man*, **24** (1924), No. 63.

203 Douglas Frazer, *Primitive Art*, London, 1962, pp. 56–59.

204 Carroll, 1967.

205 *Ibid.*, Pls. 90–94.

206 Articles on their work appear regularly in *African Arts*; see for example **1**, No. 1 (1967), pp. 16ff.: Ibrahim el Salahi; **2**, No. 1 (1968), pp. 30ff.: Felix Idubor; No. 2 (1969), pp. 34ff.: Jimo Akolo, Yusef Grillo, Ben Osawe, Erhabor Emokpae, Bruce Onobrakpeya; No. 3 (1969), pp. 18–19: Hezbon Edward Owiti; pp. 26ff.: Farid Belkahia; No. 4 (1969), pp. 20ff.: Gebre Kristos Desta, **3**, No. 1 (1969), pp. 8ff.: Nnaggenda; pp. 20ff.: Mahmoud Sehili; **3**, No. 4 (1970), pp. 8ff.: Vincent Kofi; pp. 28ff.: Francis Msanji.

207 High price of Nigerian art, *Nigeria Magazine*, **88** (1966), pp. 36–41.

208 McEwen, 1968, p. 88.

209 e.g. heads by Boira Mteki (illustrated by McEwen, 1968, p. 22) and by Richard Mteki (illustrated by Beier, 1968, Pl. 41).

210 Beier, 1968, p. 89.

211 *Ibid.*, Pls 52–54.

212 Megchelina Shore-Bos, Modern Makonde: Discovery in East African Art, *African Arts*, **3**, No. 1 (1969), pp. 46ff.; Stout, 1966.

213 His murals are in a similar style, see *African Arts*, **2**, No. 3 (1969), p. 34.

214 See Beier, 1968, Pls 3–4; Duerden, 1968, Pl. 49.

215 See Beier, 1968, Pls 92–99; Duerden, 1968, Pl. 50.

216 See Beier, 1968, Pls 77–79.

217 *Ibid.*, Pls 86–90.

218 See for example Dorothy Leadbeater, The Sicilian Cart: origins of a Western European folk art, in Smith, 1961, pp. 36–46 and discussion pp. 49ff.

219 *The Palm-wine Drinkard*, 1952; *My Life in the Bush of Ghosts*, 1954; *Simbi and the Satyr of the Dark Jungle*, 1955; *The Brave African Huntress*, 1958; and *Feather Woman of the Jungle*, 1962.

Bibliography

Akenzua, E.	1965	The Oba's Palace in Benin, *Nigeria Magazine*, **87**, pp. 244–51.
Aldred, Cyril	1949	*Old Kingdom Art in Ancient Egypt*, London.
	1961	*The Egyptians*, London/New York.
Alexandre, P. and Binet, J.	1958	*Le groupe dit Pahouin* (Ethnographic Survey of Africa) Paris.
Allison, P. A.	1944	A Yoruba carver, *Nigeria Magazine*, **22**, pp. 49–50.
	1968a	*African Stone Sculpture*, London.
	1968b	*Cross River Monoliths*, Lagos.
Bandi, H.-G., Breuil, H., Berger-Kirchner, L., Lhote, H., Holm, E. and Lommel, A.	1961	*The Art of the Stone Age*, London/New York.
Barker, Harold	1958	Radiocarbon dating: its scope and limitations, *Antiquity*, **32**, No. 194, pp. 253–63.
Bascom, William	1967	*African Arts* (Exhibition Catalogue), Berkeley, California.
	1969	*Ifa Divination: Communication between Gods and Men in West Africa*, Bloomington, Indiana.
Bastin, Marie-Louise	1961	*Art Décoratif Tshokwe*, Lisbon, 2 vols.
Beier, H. U.	1957	*The Story of Sacred Wood Carvings from one small Yoruba Town*, Lagos.
	1959	*A Year of Sacred Festivals in one Yoruba Town*, Lagos.
	1968	*Contemporary Art in Africa*, London/New York.
Biebuyck, D.	1954	Function of a Lega Mask, *Internationales Archiv für Ethnographie*, **47**, no. 1, pp. 108–20.
	1969	*Tradition and Creativity in Tribal Art*, Berkeley.
Bodrogi, T.	1968	*Art in Africa*, New York.
Boston, J. S.	1960	Some Northern Ibo masquerades, *Journal of the Royal Anthropological Institute*, **90**, Pt 1, pp. 54–65.
Brentjes, B.	1969	*African Rock Art*, London.
Carroll, K. C.	1961	Three generations of Yoruba carvers, *Ibadan*, **12**, pp. 21–24.
	1967	*Yoruba Religious Carving*, London.
Child, I. L. and Siroto, L.	1965	BaKwele and American esthetic evaluations compared, *Ethnology*, **4**, No. 4, pp. 349–60.
Cordwell, J.	1956	The problem of process and form in Yoruba art, *Proceedings of the Third International West African Conference 1949*, Lagos, pp. 53–60.
Dark, Philip	1954	*Bush Negro Art; an African Art in the Americas*, London.
Davidson, B.	1959	*Old Africa Rediscovered*, London.

d'Azevedo, Warren   1966   *The Artist Archetype in Gola Culture*
Paper presented at the Conference on the Traditional Artist in African Society, 28–30 May 1965, Tahoe Alumni Center, Lake Tahoe, California; Preprint No. 14, Desert Research Institute, University of Nevada, Reno (copy in Northwestern University Library).

Delange, Jacqueline   1967   *Arts et Peuples de l'Afrique Noire*, Paris.

Donner, E. B.   1940   Kunst und Handwerk in Nord Ost Liberia, *Baessler-Archiv*, **23**, Berlin.

Duerden, D.   1968   *African Art*, London.

Elisofon, E., and Fagg, W. B.   1958   *The Sculpture of Africa*, London/New York.

Fagg, Bernard   1956   The Nok culture, *West African Review*, 1956, pp. 1083–87.
1959   The Nok culture in prehistory, *Journal of the Historical Society of Nigeria*, **1**, 1959, pp. 288–93.
1962   The Nok terracottas in West African art history, *Actes du 4ᵉ Congrès Panafricain de Préhistoire*, Tervuren, Sect. III, pp. 445–50.
1969   Recent work in West Africa: new light on the Nok Culture, *World Archaeology*, **1**, pp. 41–50.

Fagg, William B.   1953a   *The Webster Plass Collection of African Art*, British Museum, London.
1953b   On the nature of African art, *Memoirs and Proceedings of the Manchester Literary and Philosophical Society*, **94**, pp. 93–104. (Reprinted in Legum, C.: *Africa, a handbook to the continent*, 1961, pp. 414–24.)
1955   The study of African art, *Bulletin of the Allen Memorial Art Museum*, **12**, 1955–56, pp. 44–61. *Bulletin of Oberlin College*, **14**, No. 3, pp. 44–61, 1955. Reprinted in Ottenberg, S. and P.: *Cultures and Societies of Africa*, 1960, pp. 458–73.
1959   *Afro-Portuguese Ivories*, London.
1963   *Nigerian Images*, London.
1964   *Afrika: 100 Stämme – 100 Meisterwerke*, Berlin.
1965   *Tribes and Forms in African Art*, London.
1966   *African Tribal Sculptures: I. The Niger Basin Tribes; II. The Congo Basin Tribes*, Nos. 82 and 83, Petit Encyclopédie de l'Art, Paris/New York.
1967   *The Art of Western Africa* (MQ 772, U24); *The Art of Central Africa* (MQ 773, U23), Mentor-Unesco, New York/Fontana Unesco, London.
1968   *African Tribal Images*, Cleveland, Ohio.
1970   *African Sculpture*, Washington, D.C. n.d.

Fernandez, J.   1966   Principles of opposition and vitality in Fang aesthetics, *Journal of Aesthetics and Art Criticism*, **25**, pp. 53–64.

Fischer, E.   1963   Künstler der Dan, die Bildhauer Tame, Si, Tompieme, und Sōn – ihr Wesen und ihr Werk. *Baessler-Archiv*, Neue Folge, **10**, pp. 161–263.

Forman, Werner and B. and Dark, Philip   1960   *Benin Art*, London.

Fry, Philip   1970   Essai sur la statuaire mumuye, *Objets et Mondes*, **10**, No. 1, pp. 3–28.

Gabus, Jean   1967   *Art Nègre, Recherche de ses fonctions et dimensions*, Neuchâtel.

Ganay, S. de   1941   *Les Devises des Dogons*, Travaux et Mémoires de l'Institut d'Ethnologie, Paris, **41**.

Gaskin, L. J. P.   1965   *A Bibliography of African Art*, London.

Gerbrands, A.   1957   *Art as an element of culture, especially in Negro Africa*. Mededeelingen van het Rijksmuseum voor Volkenkunde, Leiden, **12**.

Girard, J.   1967   *Dynamique de la Société Oubé*, Mémoires de l'Institut Fondamental d'Afrique Noire, **78**, Dakar.

Glück, J.	1957	Afrikanische Architektur, *Tribus*, N.F. **6**, 1956, pp. 65–82. Translated in Douglas Fraser, *The many Faces of Primitive Art: A Critical Anthology*, Englewood Cliffs, New Jersey, 1966.
Goldwater, R. J.	1938	*Primitivism in Modern Painting*, New York.
	1960	*Bambara Sculpture from the Western Sudan*, New York.
	1964	*Senufo Sculpture from West Africa*, New York.
Goodall, E., Cooke, C. K., Clark, J. D., and Summers, Roger	1959	*Prehistoric Rock Art of the Federation of Rhodesia and Nyasaland*, Salisbury, Rhodesia.
Griaule, M.	1938	*Les Masques Dogon*, Travaux et Mémoires de l'Institut d'Ethnologie, Paris, **33**, Reprinted 1963.
	1950	*Arts of the African Native*, London. (*Les Arts de l'Afrique Noire*, Paris 1947, American Edition: *Folk Arts of Black Africa*, New York, 1950.)
Harley, George W.	1950	Masks as agents of social control in Northeast Liberia, *Peabody Museum Papers*, **32**, No. 2.
Haselberger, Herta	1964	*Bautraditionen der westafrikanischen Negerkulturen*, Vienna.
Herold, E.	1967	*The Art of Africa: Tribal Masks from the Náprstek Museum, Prague*, London.
Herskovits, M. J.	1938	*Dahomey*, New York.
	1945	*Background of African Art*, Denver, Colorado.
Herskovits, M. J. and F. S.	1930	Bush Negro art, *The Arts*, October 1930.
	1934	The art of Dahomey, *American Magazine of Art*, **27**, pp. 67–76, 124–31.
Himmelheber, Hans	1935	*Negerkünstler*, Stuttgart.
	1939	Les masques Bayaka et leurs sculpteurs, *Brousse*, 1939/1, Leopoldville.
	1960	*Negerkunst und Negerkünstler*, Brunswick.
	1963	Personality and Technique of African Sculptors, *Technique and Personality*, Museum of Primitive Art, New York, Lecture Series No. 3, pp. 80–110, Greenwich, Connecticut.
	1964	Sculptors and Sculptures of the Dan, in L. Brown and M. Crowder, *Proceedings of the First International Congress of Africanists*, London, pp. 243–55.
Himmelheber, H. and V.	1958	*Die Dan*, Stuttgart.
Holas, Bahumil	1960	*Cultures Matérielles de la Côte d'Ivoire*, Paris.
Holy, Ladislav	1967	*The Art of Africa: Masks and Figures from Eastern and Southern Africa*, London.
Horton, R.	1966	*Kalabari Sculpture*, Lagos.
Hottot, R.	1956	Teke Fetishes, *Journal of the Royal Anthropological Institute*, **86**, pp. 25–36.
Keay, R. W. J.	1959	*Vegetation Map of Africa*, London.
Kjersmeier, Carl	1935–38	*Centres de style de la sculpture nègre africaine*, Paris.
Krieger, Kurt	1965/69	*Westafrikanische Plastik I, II, III*, Berlin.
Krieger, Kurt and Kutscher, Gerdt	1960	*Westafrikanische Masken*, Berlin.
Lajoux, J. D.	1963	*The Rock Paintings of Tassili*, London.
Laude, Jean	1966	*Les Arts de l'Afrique Noire*, Paris.
	1968	*La Peinture Française (1905–1914) et 'l'art nègre'. (Contribution a l'étude des sources du fauvisme et du cubisme)*, Paris.
Lebeuf, J. P.	1951	*L'Art ancien du Tchad*, *Cahiers d'Art*, 1951.
	1961	*L'Habitation des Fali, montagnards du Cameroun septentrional*, Paris.
	1962	*L'Art Ancien du Tchad; bronzes et céramiques*, Grand Palais, Paris.

Lebeuf, J. P. and Masson-Detourbet, A.	1950	*La Civilisation du Tchad*, Paris.
Lecoq, R.	1953	*Les Bamiléké*, Paris.
Leiris, Michel and Damase, J.	1959	*The Sculpture of the Tellen and the Dogon*. Hanover Gallery, London.
Leiris, Michel and Delange, Jacqueline	1967	*Afrique Noire, La Création Plastique*, Paris.
	1968	*African Art*, London (English translation of the preceding).
Lem, F. H.	1949	*Sudanese Sculptures*, Paris.
Leuzinger, E.	1960	*Africa, The Art of the Negro Peoples*, London/New York, n.d.
	1963	*African Sculpture, A Descriptive Catalogue*, Museum Rietberg, Zürich.
Lhote, Henri	1959	*The Search for the Tassili Frescoes*, London.
Libby, Willard F.	1952	*Radiocarbon Dating*, Chicago, Illinois.
von Luschan, Felix	1919	*Die Alterthümer von Benin*, 3 vols, Berlin and Leipzig.
McEwen, Frank	1968	Return to origins: new directions for African Arts, *African Arts*, **1**, No. 2, pp. 18–25, and 88.
Maesen, A.		*Umbangu, Art du Congo au Musée Royal du Congo Belge*, Tervuren.
Meauzé, Pierre	1968	*African Art: Sculpture*, Cleveland, Ohio.
Menzel, Brigitte	1968	*Goldgewichte aus Ghana*, Berlin.
Monti, Franco	1969	*African Masks*, London/New York.
Mortelmans, G. and Monteyne, R.	1962	La grotte peinte de Mbafu, témoignage iconographique de la première évangelisation du Bas-Congo. *Actes du 4ᵉ Congrès Panafricain de Préhistoire*, Tervuren, Sect. III, pp. 457–86.
Murdock, G. P.	1959	*Africa: its Peoples and their Culture History*, New York.
Obermaier, H. and Kühn, H.	1930	*Bushman Art*, London.
Ojo, G. J. A.	1966	*Yoruba Palaces*, London.
Olbrechts, F. M.	1959	*Les Arts Plastiques du Congo Belge*, Brussels/Amsterdam.
Olderogge, D. and Forman, W.	1969	*The Art of Africa: Negro Art from the Institute of Ethnography, Leningrad*. London.
Paulme, Denise	1962	*African Sculpture*, London.
Plass, Margaret	1956	*The King's Day*, Chicago (Field Museum).
Présence Africaine	1951	Présence Africaine 1951, **10–11**, *L'Art Nègre*, Paris.
Prussin, Labelle	1968	The architecture of Islam in West Africa, *African Arts*, **1**, No. 2, pp. 32–35, 70–74.
	1970a	Sudanese architecture and the Manding, *African Arts*, **3**, No. 4, pp. 12–19, 64–67.
	1970b	*Traditional Architecture in Northern Ghana*, Berkeley, California.
Rachewiltz, Boris de	1966	*Introduction to African Art*, London.
Rattray, R.	1927	*Religion and Art in Ashanti*, Oxford.
Robbins, Warren	1966	*African Art in American Collections*, New York.
Roth, H. Ling	1903	*Great Benin, Its Customs, Art and Horrors*, Halifax.
Segy, Ladislas	1952	*African Sculpture Speaks*, New York.
	1958	*African Sculpture*, New York.
Shaw, C. Thurstan	1970	*Igbo-Ukwu: An account of archaeological discoveries in eastern Nigeria*, London/Evanston, Ill.

Shinnie, Peter L.   1967   *Meroe*, London/New York.

Sieber, Roy ·   1961   *Sculpture of Northern Nigeria*, Museum of Primitive Art, New York.
                                1962   The arts and their changing social functions, *Annals of the New York Academy of Sciences*, **96**, pp. 653–58.
                                1962   Masks as agents of social control, *African Studies Bulletin*, **5**, May, No. 2, pp. 8–13.

Smith, M. W., ed.   1961   *The Artist in Tribal Society*, London.

Sousberghe, L. de   1958   *L'Art Pende*, Académie Royale de Belgique, Beaux Arts, **9**, fasc. 2.

Starkweather, Frank   1968   *Traditional Igbo Art: 1966*, Ann Arbor, Michigan.

Stout, J. A.   1966   *Modern Makonde Sculpture*, Nairobi.

Stow, George William   1905   *The Native Races of South Africa*, London.

Stow, George William and   1930   *Rock Paintings of South Africa*, London.
Bleek, Dorothea F.

Summers, R.,   1961   *Zimbabwe Excavations 1958*, Occasional Papers of the National
Robinson, K. R. and   Museums of Southern Rhodesia, **3**, No. 23 A.
Whitty, A.

Sweeney, J. J. and   1952   *African Folktales and Sculpture*, New York; 2nd edn, 1964.
Radin, P.

Swithenbank, Michael   1969   *Ashanti Fetish Houses*, Accra.

von Sydow, Eckart   1930   *Handbuch der afrikanischen Plastik, I Die westafrikanische Plastik*, Berlin.
                                1954   *Afrikanische Plastik*, ed. G. Kutscher, Berlin.

Tempels, P.   1959   *Bantu Philosophy*, Paris.

Thompson, R F   1968   Esthetics in traditional Africa, *Art News*, **66**, No. 9, pp. 44 45, 63–66.

Trowell, M.   1960   *African Design*, London.
                                1964   *Classical African Sculpture*, London, 2nd edn.

Trowell, M. and   1968   *African and Oceanic Art*, New York.
Nevermann, H.

Turnbull, Colin M.   1961   *The Forest People*, London.

Underwood, L.   1947   *Figures in Wood in West Africa*, London.
                                1948   *Masks of West Africa*, London.
                                1949   *Bronzes of West Africa*, London.

Vandenhoute, P. J. L.   1948   *Classification stylistique du masque Dan et Guéré de la Côte d'Ivoire occidentale*, Mededeelingen van het Rijksmuseum voor Volkenkunde, Leiden, **4**.

Walker Art Center   1967   *Art of the Congo*, Minneapolis, Minnesota.

Wassing, R. S.   1968   *African Art, its background and traditions*, New York.

Willcox, Alex. R.   1956   *Rock Paintings of the Drakensberg*, London.
                                1963   *The Rock Art of South Africa*, London.
                                1968   A survey of our present knowledge of rock-paintings in South Africa, *South African Archaeological Bulletin*, **23**, No. 89, pp. 20–23.

Willett, Frank   1967   *Ife in the History of West African Sculpture*, London/New York.

Willett, Frank and   1967   On the identification of individual carvers: a study of ancestor shrine
Picton, J.   carvings from Owo, Nigeria, *Man*, N.S. **2**, No. 1, pp. 62–70.

Wingert, Paul S.   1950   *The Sculpture of Negro Africa*, New York.

Acknowledgments

It is a great pleasure to acknowledge the help I have received, directly and indirectly, in the preparation of this book for in doing so I am reminded of the many friendships I have formed through the study of African art. I am indebted to Robert Plant Armstrong, Paul J. Bohannan, James D. Breckenridge and William Fagg, who kindly read the first draft of the manuscript and made most helpful suggestions; to Susannah Stevens and Luann Walther and several of her friends who at great inconvenience typed the first draft; to Esther Greene who helped in a multitude of ways to prepare the final version; to Klaus Wachsmann and Richard Wilson, my colleagues at Northwestern with whom I have had many hours of stimulating discussions; to John Picton and Roy Sieber for permission to quote their unpublished work; to William Bascom, Ulli Beier, Daniel Biebuyck, Fred Bosley, John Boston, the late R.E. Bradbury, Kevin Carroll, Desmond Clark, Justine Cordwell, Dan Crawley, Philip Dark, Oliver Davies, Jacqueline Delange, Edet Essang, Ekpo Eyo, Brian Fagan, Bernard Fagg, James Fernandez, Eberhardt Fischer, James Forde-Johnston, Douglas Fraser, Philip Fry, Adrian Gerbrands, Robert Goldwater, Marilyn Hammersley, Hans Himmelheber, Kathleen Hunt, Alan Jacobs, Kurt Krieger, Elizabeth Little, Richard Long, Brigitte Menzel, Georges Mortelmans, Peter Morton-Williams, Vicki Mundy-Castle, Kenneth Murray, Atolabi Ojo, Peter Olagunju, Hans Panofsky, Merrick Posnansky, Labelle Prussin, H. Rhotert, 'Femi Richards, Arnold Rubin, P.C. Sestieri, Leon Siroto, Edward Soja, Robert F. Thompson, Margaret Trowell, Leon Underwood, Jan Vansina, Allen Wardwell, Paul Wingert and J. Zwernemann for a wide variety of reasons. The author and publishers make grateful acknowledgment to the owners of the pieces illustrated, and to the following for photographs and drawings:

Art Institute of Chicago, 139; David Attenborough, 120; Daniel Biebuyck, 212; Ulli Beier, 248, 260, 261; the late Dr R.E. Bradbury, 87; The British Museum, 3–5, 12–14, 17–19, 47, 61, 62, 81, 92, 97, 101, 107, 115, 134–36, 150–52, 155, 160, 176–81, 183, 184, 188, 202, 203, 206, 215, 218–21, 231, 236, 237, 251; Kevin Carroll, 247, 250, 252; *Daily Times*, Lagos, 210; Philip Dark, 119; Dominique Darbois, 165, 192; Director of Museums of Southern Rhodesia, 121; Ethnological Collections of the University of Zürich, 7; The Hamlyn Group, Publishers, 257; Hans Himmelheber, 208; Photo Hoa-Qui, 105; Bayo Iribhogbe, 110–12; J.D. Lajoux, 27, 29–31; Lowie Museum of Anthropology, University of California, Berkeley, 98, 100, 149; Helen Maetzler-Prohaska, 7; Stephen Moreton-Prichard, 253; Georges Mortelmans, 36; Musée de l'Homme, Paris, 153, 187, 192, 241; Musée Royal de l'Afrique Centrale, Tervuren, 20, 93, 147, 201; Museum für Völkerkunde, Berlin, 163; Museum of Primitive Art, New York, 6; Nigerian Museum, Lagos, 66, 205, 214; G.J.A. Ojo, 117; John Picton, 207; Luigi Pigorini Museum, 60; Merrick Posnansky, 99; Labelle Prussin, 113, 114; Rietberg Museum, Zürich, 145, 146, 182; Rijksmuseum voor Volkenkunde, Leiden, 158; Robert Ritzenthaler, 106; Arnold Rubin, 51; Emil Schulthess, 26; Doig Simmonds, 258; Societé des Amis du Musée de l'Homme, 22, 213; Edward Soja, 259; Frank Speed, 244; Phillips Stevens, 235; Michelle Treiman, 209; University Museum, Philadelphia, 190; Photo S. Volta, 93; A.R. Willcox, 33, 34; Raymond Wielgus, 168; Yale University Art Gallery, 186.

All other illustrations are by the author.

Index

Figures in roman type are page numbers and indicate references in the text; those in italics are illustration numbers and indicate references in the captions; and those marked *n* refer to notes

Abeokuta 87, *1b*, *164*
Abigan, Bassi 236
aborigines, Australian 16, 31
Achebe, Chinua 172
Adesida I 129
Adewuyi, Buraima Akinlabi 235
Adugbologe *164*
aesthetics 206–22
Afenmai *1b*, *21*, *122*
Afikpo *1b*, *72*
Afo *1b*, *131*
Atonso I 65
Afro-Portuguese ivories 72, 80, 88, *53*, *55*
Agbonbiofe *116*
Ahinsan 114, *25*, *102*
Akamba *1a*, *10*
Akan *206*
Akande, Amusa 235, 236, *233*
Akanji, Adebisi 263, *260*, *261*
Akure Palace 129, *1b*, *117*
Allen, Commander William 108, *96*
Altamira 30, 45
Ambrose, Captain 232, 234, *230*, *231*
Ancient Ruins Corporation 134, 136
Ankh 114
Anyi *1a*, *206*
Apomu *1b*, *162*
Archaic Period 50
Ardra, Dahomey 81, 82, *1b*, *57*, *58*, *59*
Arman, Pierre *241*
Arowogun 228, 229, *226–28*
'art for art's sake' 164–65
artist, the individual 223–36
Ashanti 114, *1a*,
    architecture 115, 127, *115*
    art 113, 139, 241, *101–3*, *123*, *206*, *237*
Ashiru *see* Olatunde
Askia Mohammed 120
Ata of Igala *96*, *97*
Aterian complex 50

Atutu 210
Australia 16
Awka *1b*, *70*
Azande *1a*, *176–78*

BaBembe 190, *1a*, *160*
BaFumu *1a*, *150–52*
Bafut *1b*, *106*
Baga 25, *1a*, *17*, *18*
BaJokwe 194, *1a*, *61*, *62*
BaKete *1a*, *149*
BaKongo 65, 84, 245, *1a*, *35*, *60*, *159*, *239*, *241*
BaKota 190, *1a*, *182*, *183*
BaKuba 119, 192, 206, *1a*, *8*, *9*, *92*, *93*, *149*, *185*, *202*, *203*
BaKwele 216, 218, *1a*, *215*
BaLega 215, 216, 220, *1a*, *212*, *213*
Balfour, Henry 31
BaLuba 223, *1a*, *14*, *148*, *218–22*
BaLumbo 190, *1a*, *182*
BaMbala *92*, *203*
Bambara 12, 25, *1a*, *3*, *4*, *5*
Bambaraland 93
BaMbole *1a*, *20*
BaMileke *1b*, *105*, *107*
Bandele 156, 228, 229, 236, 248, *228–29*, *246–47*
Bantaji *1b*, *51*
Bantu-speaking peoples 16, 18, 58, 59, 60, 61, 206
BaPende 139, 192, 194, *1a*, *144*, *188*, *189*, *193*
BaPunu 190, *1a*, *182*
Bardai 25, 26
Barotseland 136
BaRozwi 136, *1a*, *121*
Barth, Heinrich 45
Basa Nge 197, 206, *1b*, *205*
Bascom, William R. 40, 76, *56*, *132*
BaSongye 157, *1a*, *147*, *148*, *201*
BaSuku *1a*, *146*
BaSuto 60
BaTeke 161, 168, 169, 170, *1a*, *150–52*, *192*

Battuta, Ibn 93
Bauchi *n. 57, 1b*
Baule 145, 165, 210, *1a, 136, 154, 155, 206*
BaVili *1a, 239*
BaWoyo 166, *1a, 158*
BaYaka 139, 194, *1a, 144–46*
BaYanzi *1a, 193*
Beecroft, Consul John 87, *66*
Beier, Ulli 256, 257, 259, 261, 263
Bena Lulua 192, *1a, 184*
Bende *1b, 214*
Benin art, 34, 43, 80, 96, 101, 108, 180, 253, *1b, 84–
    91, 119, 167, 169, 170, 171, 200, 251*
  Benin City 25, 27, 81, 96, 99, 101, 106, 107, 131,
    1b, 83
  King of 82, *82, 89*
  King's Palace 133, *171*
Benin Punitive Expedition (1897) 88, 101, 106, *86, 90*
Biebuyck, Daniel 40, 215, 216, *212*
Bini 81, 96, 106, *83*
Bisiri, Yemi 259, *257*
Boas, Franz 32, 33, 34, 40
Bobo *1a, 6*
Bobo Diulasso 123, *25*
Bohannan, Paul 110, 220, 221, 222
Boston, John 205
Bradbury, Dr R. E. 194, *86*
Brandberg *25, 34*
Braque, Georges 36
Brass, Niger Delta 88, *1b, 67*
Breuil, Abbé 58, 60
Bubalus Period 48, 50, 55, *26*
Buli 223, *218*
Bulom 81, *1a*
Buraimoh, Jimoh 258, *248*
Bushman 12, 15, 16, 59, 60, 61, 115, *1a, 7*
  painting 43, 56, 58, 60, *32–34*
Bushongo *91*
Bwami society 215, 220, *212, 213*

Cabinda 166, *158*
Camel period *49*
Cameroun 11, 55, 115, 119, *25, 105, 107*
Capsian 55
Carroll, Father Kevin 22, 156, 228, 229, 236, 247, 248
Cattle Period 48, 50, 53, 55, *26, 31*
cave paintings 30, 32, 43
Chad, Lake *n. 71 1b, 25*
Chamba *1b, 137*
Chariot Sub-Period 49
Chelles-Acheul complex 50
Chifubwa stream shelter 58, *25*
chi wara 12, *3*
Christianity 109, 244, 245, 248, *238, 240, 244, 247,
    250, 252*
Church Missionary Society 87
Clapperton, Commander Hugh 106
Conakry 98

Congo basin 40, 65, *214, 215*
Congo, Lower 65, 84, 161, *35, 60*
Congo river 10, 166, 190, *25*
Congo-Brazzaville 11
Congo-Kinshasa 11, 24
Cordwell, Justine 40
Crete 10, 53
Cross River area 87, *1b, 69*
Cyrenaica 53

Dahomey 11, 40, 81, 164, *23, 56–59, 157, 206*
Daima *n. 71, 1b, 25*
Dakakari 72, *1b*
Dalton, O. M. 89
Dan 165, 180, 184, 192, 211, 212, 226, *1a, 174, 175,
    186, 208, 223–25*
Dapper, Olfert 101, 102, 108, *83, 84*
D'Azevedo, Warren 215
DeBry, J. T. 101
degeneration theory 31
Delange, Jacqueline 41
Derain, André 35, 145, *22, 192*
Dieterlen, Germaine 40
Dixon, R. B. 32
Djenne 120, 123, *25*
Dogon 40, 41, 77, 120, 123, 156, 157, 168, 193, *1a, 47,
    110, 111, 187, 190*
Drakensberg 60, *25, 33*
Duala *1b, 206*

Edo 127, 197, *1b, 25*
Efik 92, *1b*
Efon Alaye *1b, 116*
egungun 76, 173–74, *163, 164, 166*
Egypt 10, 40, 53, 65, 109, 110, 112, 114, 244, *98, 100*
Einstein, Carl 34
Ekiti 152, 236, 248, *1b, 28, 245–46*
Ekoi *1b, 66, 69*
Ekwensi, Cyprian 254
El Ahaiwah *25, 100*
Elisofon, Eliot 40
Engaruka *136, 25*
Ennedi Plateau 50, *25*
Enwonwu, Ben 253, 264, *252*
Enyong Division *1b, 52*
Eshure 50, *1b, 28*
Esie 72, *1b*
Ethiopia 18, 244

Fadioute, Senegal 246, *25, 238*
Fagg, Bernard 40, *73*
Fagg, William 5, 18, 40, 88, 106, 108, 152, 188, 200,
    226, *48, 49, 84, 112, 171*
Fakeye, Ganiyu 235, 236, *233*
Fakeye, Joseph 228, 235, 236, *229, 233*
Fakeye, Lamidi *see* Lamidi
Fali 115, *1b*
Fang 162, 218, 220, *1a, 22, 153*
Fanti 222, *103*

Fernandez, James 40, 162, 218, 220
Fezzan 45, 55, 25
Fischer, E. 40, 212, 226, 228
Fon 40, 164, 1b, 157, 206
Fouta Toro 56, 25
France 32
Franco–Cantabrian rock art 72
Frobenius, Leo 35, 92, 129, 163, 236
Froger, François 98, 80, 81
frontality 110, 144, 220
Fulani 55, 56, 1a, 1b
function of art 164–69

Gabon 11, 36, 162
Gambia river 98, 25, 80
Ganay, Solange de 40
Gao 120, 25
Gauguin, Paul 35
!Gcu-Wa 56
gelede 69, 87, 197, 38, 65
Gerbrands, Adrian 31, 41, 166, 211
Ghana 25, 62
Ghana, ancient 24
Girard, Jean 188
Glover, Governor John H. 87, 65
Glück, Julius 115, 127
Gola 215, 1a
Goodwin, John 102
Gor society 184, 185
Griaule, Marcel 25, 40, 43, 110
Gris, Juan 36, 183
growth curves 200–06
Guinea 11, 26, 174, 180, 192
Gulome 211
Guro 69, 98, 210, 1a, 81

Haddon, A.C. 31
Ham 72, 116, 120, 1b
Haselberger, Herta 115
Hassi Meniet 52
Hausa 119, 1b
Henrique, Don 65, 36
Herodotus 53
Herskovits, Melville 40, 157
Himmelheber, Hans 40, 69, 165, 184, 185, 210, 155
Hirschberg, Walter 99
Hoggar 50, 52, 53, 25
Holmes, W.H. 31
Holy, Ladislav 18
Horn of Africa 11, 239, 25
Horse and Camel Sub-Period 49
Horse Period 49
Horseman Sub-Period 49
Horton, Robin 161, 172, 174, 177, 180
Hottentot 58, 59, 60, 99, 1a
Hottot, Robert 161, 168, 170, 150–52

Ibadan 235, 250, 257, 1b, 198, 199
ibeji 87, 144, 169, 68, 133, 209, 233

Ibibio 73, 92, 194, 197, 1b, 124–26, 191, 194–96, 199
Ibo 180, 220, 222, 1b, 70–76, 172, 173, 197, 204
Idah, Ata of 108, 1b, 96, 97
Idoma 1b, 197
Idubor, Felix 264
Ifa divination 82, n. 76, 56, 59, 140, 141
Ife 26, 43, 72, 73–76, 128, 169, 170, 229, 1b, 23, 24, 28, 40–42, 45, 63, 91, 161, 229
Igala 1b, 76–79, 96, 97
Igbira 197, 206, 208, 1b, 205, 207
Igbo-Ukwu 73, 1b, 43, 44
Ihiovi, Amodu 206, 208, 205, 207
Ijebu 25, 82, 236, 1b
Ijo 92, 1b, 67, 90, 138, 167, 168
ikenga 74, 75, 76
Ikere 234, 1b, 231
Ikot Ekpene 194, 197, 1b, 191, 194, 199
Ila 228, 1b, 166, 209, 210
Ilaje 165, 1b, 90
Ilaro 88, 1b, 68
Ilesha 76, 232, 1b, 15, 16, 46
Ilorin 127, 1b, 118
impluvium 127, 128, 129, 131, 133, 116, 119
Indians, North American 16, 32
Initinen 53
Inyanga Mountains 136, 25
iroko wood 18, 156
Ise 232, 230–34
Ishan 194, 197, 1b, 194, 198, 199
Islam 26, 93, 109, 120–27, 239, 241, 244, 108, 109, 112–14, 118, 234, 236
Ita Yemoo 72, 42
Ituri forest 24, 25
Ivory Coast 26, 123, 180, 192, 211, 174, 175

Jaba, see Ham
Jebba 1b, 50
Jebel Uweinat 50, 25
Jos 172, 1b, 104
Jukun 1b, 51, 129

Kalabari Ijo 41, 161, 174, 177, 180, 1b, 167, 168
Kalahari Desert 11, 15, 58, 25
Kawara 125, 25, 114
Kenya 17, 64, 25
Ketu 1b, 23
Khami Ruins 136, 25
Kilwa Island 120, 25
King Solomon's Mines 133
Kissi 98, 174, 1a
Kjersmeier, C. 37, 92, 111
Kolb, Peter 99
Kong 123, 125, 25
Kongo, Kingdom of 245
Kran 180
Kroeber, A.L. 32
Kuchamfa 68, 1b
Kurumba 25, 1a

Lagos 40, 87, 197, 226, 254, *1b*, *252*
Lajoux, J.-D. *27*
Lamidi 228, 229, 235, 236, 248, 250, 251, *229*, *233*, *244*
Lander, Richard 108
Lapai *1b*, *235*
Laude, Jean 36
Lebeuf, J. P. 40
Le Corbusier 116
Leiris, Michel 36, 41
Lem, F. H. 40
Lemaire 99
Leonardo da Vinci 27
Levallois-Mousterian complex 52
Lhote, Henri 50, 55
Liberia 26, 192, 212, 215, 226, *174*, *175*
Libyans 53
Limpopo 136, *25*
Lobi *1a*, *19*
Lome 211
Los, Isles of 96, *25*
Lower Niger Bronze Industries *48*, *49*
Lowie, R. H. 32
Loyer, Godefroy 99
Lozi *1a*, *12*
Lugard, Lord 247
Luschan, F. von 101

Mada *1b*, *104*
Madagascar 11
Maesen, A. 40
Magbwe, Uwi 211
Maillol, Aristide 36
MaKaranga 134, *1a*
MaKonde 258, *1a*, *13*
Mali Empire 93, 120
Malli 93
Mama *1b*, *127*, *128*
Mangbetu *1a*, *179–81*
Mansa Musa 120
Marees, Pieter de 101, *82*
Masai 17, *1a*
MaShona 134, *1a*, *11*
masks 55, 172–208, *5*, *6*, *14*, *17*, *22*, *26*, *40*, *54*, *65*, *72*,
    73, *77–79*, *81*, *90*, *126*, *130*, *139*, *145–49*, *155*,
    165, *172–75*, *182*, *191*, *192*, *204–5*, *207*, *223–25*,
    236, *242*, *243*
Matisse, Henri 35, *22*
Mauritania 49, 50, *25*
Mauss, Marcel 41
Mbafu 64, 84, 245, *25*, *36*
Mbari Mbayo 257, 258, 259, 263, 264, *248*, *254*, *257–
    61*
Mbour *25*, *234*
McEwen, Frank 254, 256, *n. 9*
Meko *1b*, *38*
Mende *98*, *1a*, *54*
Modakeke section of Ife 76, *24*
Modigliani, Amadeo 145

Mokwa *1b*, *236*
Monomotapa 134
Montol 226
Mopti 123, *25*, *112*
Mozambique 43
Mpongwe *1a*, *182*
Mugabe 136
Mukomberanwa, Nicholas *253*
Mumuye *1b*, *137*
Murray, Kenneth 40, 165, 172, 226

Nachikufan complex 58, 59
Nachikufu *25*
Nag'ed Deir *25*, *98*
Nakapapula 58, *25*
Naletale 136, *25*, *121*
NDengese *1a*, *93*
Ndonc, Laurent 246, *238*
Ngbula play 180
Ngere *174*, 180, 188, 192, *1a*, *165*, *186*
Nguni 136
Niger 12
Niger river 77, 88, 96, 120, 161, 172, 180, 194, *1b*, *25*,
    110
Nigeria 24, 28, 37, 40, 50, 65, 72, 73, 115, 119, 127,
    226, 239, 247, 264, *1b*, *25*
Nok 24, 40, 65, 68, 69, 72, 73, 75, 116, 164, *1b*, *37–39*,
    156
nomoli figures 72, 80, 98, *53*
Nubia 120, 244, *25*
Nupe 120, 239, 241, *1b*, *50*, *235*, *236*
Nyani 93, *25*
Nyendael, David 102, 106, 108
Nyero *25*, *99*

Oba Akenzua II, King of Benin *89*
Obaloran, Chief 169, *161*
Obalufon *40*
Obatala *142*, *143*
Obo-Ekiti 259
Ockiya, King 88, *67*
Odo Owa *1b*, *242–43*
Ogbomosho *1b*, *211*
Ogboni 169, 248, 259, *162*, *245*, *246*
Oghiamien, Chief 133, *119*, *200*
Ogoni *1b*, *124–26*, *130*
Ogowe river 190, *25*
Ojo, G. J. A. 129
Olaniyi, Taiwo 257, *254*
Olatunde, Ashiru 261, *258*
Olbrechts, F. M. 37, 40, 190, 194, 226
Old Calabar *1b*, *66*
Old Obo *1b*, *255–57*
Old Oyo 107, *1b*, *94*, *95*
Old Somorika *1b*, *122*
Olowe of Ise 232, 234, *230–32*
O'Mahoney, Father 247
Ona, Thomas *132*

286

Ondo Province 232
Onipasanobe 88
Onitsha *1b*, *172*
Onobrakpeya, Bruce 254, *249*
Op Art 157
Opobo *1b*, *124–25*
Oran 45, 55, *25*
Orisha Iko cult 169, *161*
Oro 228
Oshamuko 228, 229, *227*, *228*
Oshogbo 257, 261, 263, *1b*, *258–61*; *see also* Mbari
   Mbayo
Oshun 263, *259*, *261*
Osi Ekiti 228, 229, *1b*, *245*
Osifo, Osagie 253, 264, *250*
Owerri *1b*, *173*
Owo 82, 237, *1b*, *64*
Oyate *1b*, *242*
Oye Ekiti 247, 250, 252, 253
Oyo 107, 144, *1b*, *94*, *95*

Paulme, Denise 40
Pereira, Pacheco 80, 96, 98
Perry, W.J. 109
Phillipp Cave 58
Picasso, Pablo 35, 145, 254, *22*, *213*
Picton, John 76, 197, 206, 237, *68*
Pitt-Rivers, A.H. Lane-Fox 31, 89
Pleistocene, Upper 59
pomdo 98
Poro society 26, 192, *174*, *175*
Portugal 80, 245
Portuguese 64, 80, 81, *169*
primitive art 27–28
proportions 35, 161–64
proverb pot-lids 166–68, *158*
Prussin, Labelle 120, 241, *112*
Pygmies 15, 16, 24, *115*, *1a*

Read, C.H. 89
Rhodesia 133, 136, 254, 256
Robinson, K.R. 134
rock painting 12, 17, 43–58, 245
Rome 84
Roth, H. Ling 89, 102
Rubin, Arnold *51*
Ryder, Alan 80, 81

Sahara 10, 11, 12, 17, 24, 45, 48, 49, 50, 52, 53, 55, 56,
   110, *25*
Sakiwa *235*
Salisbury, Rhodesia 254, 256, *n. 9*, *25*, *253*
Sanga *110*, *111*
Sankore 120, *113*
de Sautuola 45
Sayce, R.U. 34
Schmidt, Max 31
Schüz, Georg Emil 88, *68*
Segu *4*, *5*, *25*

Semper, Gottfried 30, 31
Senegal 55, 56, 246
Senufo *1a*, *134*, *135*, *139*
setting of African sculpture 169–88
Shamba Balongongo *92*
Shaw, Thurstan 73, *43*
Sheba, Queen of 134
Sherbro 72, 80, *1a*
Shongo 87, *94*, *211*
Si 226
Sieber, Roy 226, 241
Sierra Leone 26, 72, 80, 192, *53*, *54*
Siroto, Leon 216, *183*
S.M.A. fathers 247
Smith, G. Elliot 109
Soku 172
Somalia 64, *25*
Sōn 226
Songhay 24, 120, *25*
Spain 59
Stanley Falls 10, *25*
Stolpe, Hjalmar 31
Stow, G.W. 56
Strabo 53
style 188–208
Sudan 11, 40, 120, 239, *25*
Sumerians 60
Summers, Roger 134
Swithenbank 127
Switzerland *87*
Sydow, Eckart von 36, 37

Tame 226, *223*, *224*
Tanganyika 17
Tanzania 64, 136, *25*
Taruga 68, *1b*
Tassili 45, 50, 52, 53, 55, 56, 68, 146, *25*, *27*, *29–31*
Tellem 77, *47*
Temne 81, *1a*
Tempels, Fr Placide 206
Ténéré 12, *25*
Thompson, Robert 88, 212, 215
Tibesti 50, *25*
Timbuktu 45, 120, 123, *25*, *113*
Titerast-n'-Elias 52, 53
Tiv 72, 115, 220, 222, *1b*, *216*, *217*
Togo 11
Tompieme 212, 226, 227, *208*, *225*
Tripoli 45, *25*
Trowell, Margaret 34, 41, 109, 139, 177
Tucker, Reeve 232, *230*
Tunisia 55, *25*
Turnbull, Colin 24
Tutuola, Amos 258, 264
Twins Seven Seven 257, *254*

Uganda 64, *25*
Ughoton *1b*, *90*

Uhlman, Fred 145, 146
Underwood, Leon 146
Upper Cavally river 180
Urhobo 150, *1b*, *138*
U.S.A. 10, 32

Vandenhoute, P. J. L. 40, 180, 185, 188, 193, 205, 211,
    212
Vatter, E. 36
Victoria Falls 10, *25*
Victoria, Lake 110, *25*
Vissers, Fathers Frans and Jan 166
Vlaminck, Maurice 35, *22*
Vollard, Ambroise 35
Volta river 120, 123

Wadi Djerat 48
Wamba 164, *1b*, *156*
Welsh, James 81
Wenger, Susanne 259, 261, 263, *259*
'White Lady of the Brandberg' 60, *34*
Whitty, Anthony 134, 135
Wieckmann collection 81, *55*, *57–59*

Willcox, A. R. 56, 58, 60
Willett, Frank 237
Windhoek 58, *25*
Wingert, Paul S. 37, 139
·Wissler, Clark 32
Witteberge *25*, *32*
Wobe 180, 188, *1a*
Wolfe, Alvin 42
Worringer, Wilhelm 32
Wukari *1b*, *51*

Yacuba 188
Yituwo 211
Yoruba 22, 41, 50, 69, 72, 76, 81, 87, 107, 127, 129,
    156, 165, 168, 173, 197, 212, 213, 215, 216, 222,
    228, 229, *1b*, *15*, *16*, *38*, *45*, *46*, *56–59*, *63–65*, *68*,
    92, *94*, *95*, *116–18*, *132*, *133*, *140–43*, *162–64*,
    166, *209–11*, *226–33*, *242–47*, *257*

Zambesi 10, 136, *25*
Zambia 58, 64, *25*
Zaria 65, *1b*, *108*, *109*
Zimbabwe 133, 134–36, *25*, *120*
Zulu 8, *1b*, *13*